T0210727

Beginning Functional JavaScript

Uncover the Concepts of Functional Programming with EcmaScript 8

Second Edition

Anto Aravinth
Srikanth Machiraju

Apress®

Beginning Functional JavaScript

Anto Aravinth
Chennai, Tamil Nadu, India

Srikanth Machiraju
Hyderabad, Andhra Pradesh, India

ISBN-13 (pbk): 978-1-4842-4086-1
https://doi.org/10.1007/978-1-4842-4087-8

ISBN-13 (electronic): 978-1-4842-4087-8

Library of Congress Control Number: 2018964615

Copyright © Anto Aravinth, Srikanth Machiraju 2018, corrected publication 2020

This work is subject to copyright. All rights are reserved by the Publisher, whether the whole or part of the material is concerned, specifically the rights of translation, reprinting, reuse of illustrations, recitation, broadcasting, reproduction on microfilms or in any other physical way, and transmission or information storage and retrieval, electronic adaptation, computer software, or by similar or dissimilar methodology now known or hereafter developed.

Trademarked names, logos, and images may appear in this book. Rather than use a trademark symbol with every occurrence of a trademarked name, logo, or image we use the names, log os, and images only in an editorial fashion and to the benefit of the trademark owner, with no intention of infringement of the trademark.

The use in this publication of trade names, trademarks, service marks, and similar terms, even if they are not identified as such, is not to be taken as an expression of opinion as to whether or not they are subject to proprietary rights.

While the advice and information in this book are believed to be true and accurate at the date of publication, neither the authors nor the editors nor the publisher can accept any legal responsibility for any errors or omissions that may be made. The publisher makes no warranty, express or implied, with respect to the material contained herein.

Managing Director, Apress Media LLC: Welmoed Spahr
Acquisitions Editor: Nikhil Karakal
Development Editor: Matthew Moodie
Coordinating Editor: Divya Modi

Cover designed by eStudioCalamar

Cover image designed by Freepik (www.freepik.com)

Distributed to the book trade worldwide by Springer Science+Business Media New York, 233 Spring Street, 6th Floor, New York, NY 10013. Phone 1-800-SPRINGER, fax (201) 348-4505, e-mail orders-ny@springer-sbm.com, or visit www.springeronline.com. Apress Media, LLC is a California LLC and the sole member (owner) is Springer Science + Business Media Finance Inc (SSBM Finance Inc). SSBM Finance Inc is a Delaware corporation.

For information on translations, please e-mail rights@apress.com, or visit http://www.apress. com/rights-permissions.

Apress titles may be purchased in bulk for academic, corporate, or promotional use. eBook versions and licenses are also available for most titles. For more information, reference our Print and eBook Bulk Sales web page at http://www.apress.com/bulk-sales.

Any source code or other supplementary material referenced by the author in this book is available to readers on GitHub via the book's product page, located at www.apress.com/. For more detailed information, please visit http://www.apress.com/source-code.

Printed on acid-free paper

Table of Contents

About the Authors

Anto Aravinth has been in the software industry for more than six years. He has developed many systems that are written in the latest technologies. Anto has knowledge of the fundamentals of JavaScript and how it works and has trained many people. Anto is also does OSS in his free time and loves to play table tennis.

Srikanth Machiraju has over ten years of experience as a developer, architect, technical trainer, and community speaker. He is currently working as Senior Consultant with Microsoft Hyderabad, leading a team of 100 developers and quality analysts developing an advanced cloud-based platform for a tech giant in the oil industry. With an aim to be an enterprise architect who can design hyperscale modern applications with intelligence, he constantly learns and shares modern application development tactics using cutting-edge platforms and technologies. Prior to Microsoft, he worked with BrainScale as Corporate Trainer and Senior Technical Analyst on application design, development, and migrations using Azure. He is a tech-savvy developer who is passionate about embracing new technologies and sharing his learning via blog and community engagements. He has also authored the "Learning Windows Server Containers" and "Developing Bots with Microsoft Bot Framework," blogs at `https://vishwanathsrikanth.wordpress.com`. He runs his own YouTube channel called "Tech Talk with Sriks" and is active on LinkedIn at `https://www.linkedin.com/in/vishsrik/`.

About the Technical Reviewer

 **Sakib Shaikh** has been working as a Tech Lead with a large scientific publisher, with more than ten years of experience as a full stack developer with JavaScript technologies on front-end and back-end systems. He has been reviewing technical books and articles for the past few years and contributes to the developer community as a trainer, blogger, and mentor.

Acknowledgments

I remember the first code that I wrote for Juspay Systems in my first job as an intern. Coding was fun for me; at times it is challenging, too. Now with six years of software experience, I want to make sure I pass on all the knowledge I have to the community. I love teaching people. I love to share my thoughts with the community to get feedback. That's exactly the reason I'm writing a second edition of this book.

I have to acknowledge few people who have been standing right next to me in all phases of my life: my late father Belgin Rayen, mother Susila, Kishore (brother-in-law), Ramya (sibling), and Joshuwa (my new little nephew). They have been supportive and pushed me harder to achieve my goals. I want to say thanks to Divya and the technical reviewer of this book, as they did a wonderful job. Luckily, I have a wonderful coauthor in Srikanth, who did an amazing job as well.

Finally, I want to give special thanks to Bianaca, Deepak, Vishal, Arun, Vishwapriya, and Shabala, who have added joy to my life.

Please reach out to me at `anto.aravinth.cse@gmail.com` with any feedback.

—Anto Aravinth

I would like to thank Apress for providing me a second opportunity to author. I would also like to thank my family, especially my dear wife Sonia Madan and my four-month-old son Reyansh for supporting me throughout this stint. I'm always reachable at `Vishwanath.srikanth@gmail.com` for any feedback or questions.

—Srikanth Machiraju

Introduction

The second edition of a book is always special. When I wrote the first edition, I had about two years of IT experience. The book received positive as well as negative responses. I always wanted to work on the negative responses to make the content better and make the book worth the price. In the meantime, JavaScript evolved a great deal. Many ground-breaking changes were added into the language. The Web is full of JavaScript, and imagine a world without the Web. Hard, right?

This second edition is a much improved version that teaches the fundamentals of functional programming in JavaScript. We have added much new content in this second edition; for example, we will be building a library for building web applications using functional concepts, and we have added sections on testing as well. We have rewritten the book to match the latest ES8 syntax with many samples of async, await patterns, and a lot more!

We assure you that you will gain a lot of knowledge from this book and at the same time you will have fun while running the examples. Start reading.

CHAPTER 1

Functional Programming in Simple Terms

The first rule of functions is that they should be small. The second rule of functions is that they should be smaller than that.

—Robert C. Martin

Welcome to the functional programming world, a world that has only functions, living happily without any outside world dependencies, without states, and without mutations—forever. Functional programming is a buzzword these days. You might have heard about this term within your team or in a local group meeting. If you're already aware of what that means, great. For those who don't know the term, don't worry. This chapter is designed to introduce you to *functional* terms in simple English.

We are going to begin this chapter by asking a simple question: What is a function in mathematics? Later, we are going to create a function in JavaScript with a simple example using our function definition. The chapter ends by explaining the benefits that functional programming provides to developers.

© Anto Aravinth, Srikanth Machiraju 2018
A. Aravinth and S. Machiraju, *Beginning Functional JavaScript*,
https://doi.org/10.1007/978-1-4842-4087-8_1

What Is Functional Programming? Why Does It Matter?

Before we begin to explore what functional programming means, we have to answer another question: What is a function in mathematics? A function in mathematics can be written like this:

$$f(X) = Y$$

The statement can be read as "A function f, which takes X as its argument, and returns the output Y." X and Y can be any number, for instance. That's a very simple definition. There are key takeaways in the definition, though:

- A function must always take an argument.

- A function must always return a value.

- A function should act only on its receiving arguments (i.e., X), not the outside world.

- For a given X, there will be only one Y.

You might be wondering why we presented the definition of function in mathematics rather than in JavaScript. Did you? That's a great question. The answer is pretty simple: Functional programming techniques are heavily based on mathematical functions and their ideas. Hold your breath, though; we are not going to teach you functional programming in mathematics, but rather use JavaScript. Throughout the book, however, we will be seeing the ideas of mathematical functions and how they are used to help understand functional programming.

With that definition in place, we are going to see the examples of functions in JavaScript. Imagine we have to write a function that does tax calculations. How are you going to do this in JavaScript? We can implement such a function as shown in Listing 1-1.

Listing 1-1. Calculate Tax Function

```
var percentValue = 5;
var calculateTax = (value) => { return value/100 * (100 +
percentValue) }
```

The `calculateTax` function does exactly what we want to do. You can call this function with the value, which will return the calculated tax value in the console. It looks neat, doesn't it? Let's pause for a moment and analyze this function with respect to our mathematical definition. One of the key points of our mathematical function term is that the function logic shouldn't depend on the outside world. In our `calculateTax` function, we have made the function depend on the *global* variable `percentValue`. Thus this function we have created can't be called as a real function in a mathematical sense. Let's fix that.

The fix is very straightforward: We have to just move the `percentValue` as our function argument, as shown in Listing 1-2.

Listing 1-2. Rewritten `calculateTax` Function

```
var calculateTax = (value, percentValue) => { return value/100 *
(100 + percentValue) }
```

Now our `calculateTax` function can be called as a real function. What have we gained, though? We have just eliminated global variable access inside our `calculateTax` function. Removing global variable access inside a function makes it easy for testing. (We will talk about the functional programming benefits later in this chapter.)

Now we have shown the relationship between the math function and our JavaScript function. With this simple exercise, we can define functional programming in simple technical terms. Functional programming is a paradigm in which we will be creating functions that are going to work out their logic by depending only on their input. This ensures that a function, when called multiple times, is going to return the same result. The function also won't change any data in the outside world, leading to a cachable and testable code base.

FUNCTIONS VS. METHODS IN JAVASCRIPT

We have talked about the word *function* a lot in this text. Before we move on, we want to make sure you understand the difference between functions and methods in JavaScript.

Simply put, a *function* is a piece of code that can be called by its name. It can be used to pass arguments that it can operate on and return values optionally.

A *method* is a piece of code that must be called by its name that is associated with an object.

Listing 1-3 and Listing 1-4 provide quick examples of a function and a method.

Listing 1-3. A Simple Function

```
var simple = (a) => {return a} // A simple function
simple(5) //called by its name
```

Listing 1-4. A Simple Method

```
var obj = {simple : (a) => {return a} }
obj.simple(5) //called by its name along with its associated
object
```

There are two more important characteristics of functional programming that are missing in the definition. We discuss them in detail in the upcoming sections before we dive into the benefits of functional programming.

Referential Transparency

With our definition of function, we have made a statement that all the functions are going to return the same value for the same input. This property of a function is called a *referential transparency*. A simple example is shown in Listing 1-5.

Listing 1-5. Referential Transparency Example

```
var identity = (i) => { return i }
```

In Listing 1-5, we have defined a simple function called `identity`. This function is going to return whatever you're passing as its input; that is, if you're passing 5, it's going to return the value 5 (i.e., the function just acts as a mirror or identity). Note that our function operates only on the incoming argument `i`, and there is no global reference inside our function (remember in Listing 1-2, we removed `percentValue` from global access and made it an incoming argument). This function satisfies the conditions of a referential transparency. Now imagine this function is used between other function calls like this:

```
sum(4,5) + identity(1)
```

With our referential transparency definition, we can convert that statement into this:

```
sum(4,5) + 1
```

Now this process is called a *substitution model* as you can directly substitute the result of the function as is (mainly because the function doesn't depend on other global variables for its logic) with its value. This leads to *parallel* code and *caching*. Imagine that with this model, you can easily run the given function with multiple threads without even the need to synchronize. Why? The reason for synchronizing comes from the fact that threads shouldn't act on global data when running parallel.

Functions that obey referential transparency are going to depend only on inputs from their argument; hence threads are free to run without any locking mechanism.

Because the function is going to return the same value for the given input, we can, in fact cache it. For example, imagine there is a function called `factorial`, which calculates the factorial of the given number. `Factorial` takes the input as its argument for which the factorial needs to be calculated. We know the factorial of 5 is going to be 120. What if the user calls the factorial of 5 a second time? If the `factorial` function obeys referential transparency, we know that the result is going to be 120 as before (and it only depends on the input argument). With this characteristic in mind, we can cache the values of our `factorial` function. Thus if `factorial` is called for a second time with the input as 5, we can return the cached value instead of calculating it once again.

Here you can see how a simple idea helps in parallel code and cachable code. We will be writing a function in our library for caching the function results later in the chapter.

REFERENTIAL TRANSPARENCY IS A PHILOSOPHY

Referential transparency is a term that came from analytic philosophy (https://en.wikipedia.org/wiki/Analytical_philosophy). This branch of philosophy deals with natural language semantics and its meanings. Here the word *referential* or *referent* means the thing to which the expression refers. A context in a sentence is referentially transparent if replacing a term in that context with another term that refers to the same entity doesn't alter the meaning.

That's exactly how we have been defining referential transparency here. We have replaced the value of the function without affecting the context.

Imperative, Declarative, Abstraction

Functional programming is also about being *declarative* and writing *abstracted* code. We need to understand these two terms before we proceed further. We all know and have worked on an imperative paradigm. We'll take a problem and see how to solve it in an imperative and declarative fashion.

Suppose you have a list or array and want to iterate through the array and print it to the console. The code might look like Listing 1-6.

Listing 1-6. Iterating over the Array Imperative Approach

```
var array = [1,2,3]
for(i=0;i<array.length;i++)
    console.log(array[i]) //prints 1, 2, 3
```

It works fine. In this approach to solve our problem, though, we are telling exactly "how" we need to do it. For example, we have written an implicit for loop with an index calculation of the array length and printing the items. We will stop here. What was the task here? Print the array elements, right? It looks like we are telling the compiler what to do, however. In this case, we are telling the compiler, "Get array length, loop our array, get each element of the array using the index, and so on." We call it an imperative solution. *Imperative* programming is all about telling the compiler how to do things.

We will now switch to the other side of the coin, *declarative* programming. In declarative programming, we are going to tell what the compiler needs to do rather than how. The "how" parts are abstracted into common functions (these functions are called higher order functions, which we cover in the upcoming chapters). Now we can use the built-in forEach function to iterate the array and print it, as shown in Listing 1-7.

Listing 1-7. Iterating over the Array Declarative Approach

```
var array = [1,2,3]
array.forEach((element) => console.log(element))
//prints 1, 2, 3
```

Listing 1-7 does print exactly the same output as Listing 1-5. Here, though, we have removed the "how" parts like "Get array length, loop our array, get each element of an array using an index, and so on." We have used an abstracted function, which takes care of the "how" part, leaving us, the developers, to worry about our problem at hand (the "what" part). We will be creating these built-in functions throughout the book.

Functional programming is about creating functions in an abstracted way that can be reused by other parts of the code. Now we have a solid understanding of what functional programming is; with this in mind, we can explore the benefits of functional programming.

Functional Programming Benefits

We have seen the definition of functional programming and a very simple example of a function in JavaScript. We now have to answer a simple question: What are the benefits of functional programming? This section helps you see the huge benefits that functional programming offers us. Most of the benefits of functional programming come from writing pure functions. So before we see the benefits of functional programming, we need to know what a pure function is.

Pure Functions

With our definition in place, we can define what is meant by pure functions. *Pure functions* are the functions that return the same output for the given input. Take the example in Listing 1-8.

Listing 1-8. A Simple Pure Function

```
var double = (value) => value * 2;
```

This function double is a pure function because given an input, it is always going to return the same output. You can try it yourself. Calling the double function with input 5 always gives the result as 10. Pure functions obey referential transparency. Thus we can replace double(5) with 10, without any hesitations.

So what's the big deal about pure functions? They provide many benefits, which we discuss next.

Pure Functions Lead to Testable Code

Functions that are not pure have side effects. Take our previous tax calculation example from Listing 1-1:

```
var percentValue = 5;
var calculateTax = (value) => { return value/100 * (100 +
percentValue) } //depends on external environment percentValue
variable
```

The function calculateTax is not a pure function, mainly because for calculating its logic it depends on the external environment. The function works, but it is very difficult to test. Let's see the reason for this.

Imagine we are planning to run a test for our calculateTax function three times for three different tax calculations. We set up the environment like this:

```
calculateTax(5) === 5.25
```

```
calculateTax(6) === 6.3
```

```
calculateTax(7) === 7.350000000000005
```

The entire test passed. However, because our original `calculateTax` function depends on the external environment variable `percentValue`, things can go wrong. Imagine the external environment is changing the `percentValue` variable while you are running the same test cases:

```
calculateTax(5) === 5.25
```

```
// percentValue is changed by other function to 2
calculateTax(6) === 6.3   //will the test pass?
```

```
// percentValue is changed by other function to 0
calculateTax(7) === 7.3500000000000005 //will the test pass or
throw exception?
```

As you can see here, the function is very hard to test. We can easily fix the issue, though, by removing the external environment dependency from our function, leading the code to this:

```
var calculateTax = (value, percentValue) => { return value/100
* (100 + percentValue) }
```

Now you can test this function without any pain. Before we close this section, we need to mention an important property about pure functions: Pure functions also shouldn't mutate any external environment variables. In other words, the pure function shouldn't depend on any external variables (as shown in the example) and also change any external variables. We'll now take a quick look what we mean by changing any external variables. For example, consider the code in Listing 1-9.

Listing 1-9. badFunction Example

```
var global = "globalValue"
var badFunction = (value) => { global = "changed";
return value * 2 }
```

When the badFunction function is called it changes the global variable global to the value changed. Is it something to worry about? Yes. Imagine another function that depends on the global variable for its business logic. Thus, calling badFunction affects other functions' behavior. Functions of this nature (i.e., functions that have side effects) make the code base hard to test. Apart from testing, these side effects will make the system behavior very hard to predict in the case of debugging.

So we have seen with a simple example how a pure function can help us in easily testing the code. Now we'll look at other benefits we get out of pure functions: reasonable code.

Reasonable Code

As developers we should be good at reasoning about the code or a function. By creating and using pure functions we can achieve that very simply. To make this point clearer, we are going to use a simple example of function double (from Listing 1-8):

```
var double = (value) => value * 2
```

Looking at this function name, we can easily reason that this function doubles the given number and nothing else. In fact, using our referential transparency concept, we can easily go ahead and replace the double function call with the corresponding result. Developers spend most of their time reading others' code. Having a function with side effects in your code base makes it hard for other developers in your team to read. Code bases with pure functions are easy to read, understand, and test. Remember that a function (regardless of whether it is a pure function) must always have a meaningful name. For example, you can't name the function double as dd given what it does.

SMALL MIND GAME

We are just replacing the function with a value, as if we know the result without seeing its implementation. That's a great improvement in your thinking process about functions. We are substituting the function value as if that's the result it will return.

To give your mind a quick exercise, see this reasoning ability with our in-built `Math.max` function.

Given the function call:

`Math.max(3,4,5,6)`

What will be the result?

Did you see the implementation of `max` to give the result? No, right? Why? The answer to that question is `Math.max` is a pure function. Now have a cup of coffee; you have done a great job!

Parallel Code

Pure functions allow us to run the code in parallel. As a pure function is not going to change any of its environments, this means we do not need to worry about *synchronizing* at all. Of course JavaScript doesn't have real threads to run the functions in parallel, but what if your project uses WebWorkers for running multiple things in parallel? Or a server-side code in a node environment that runs the function in parallel?

For example, imagine we have the code given in Listing 1-10.

Listing 1-10. Impure Functions

```
let global = "something"
let function1 = (input) => {
        // works on input
        //changes global
        global = "somethingElse"
}
let function2 = () => {
        if(global === "something")
        {
                //business logic
        }
}
```

What if we need to run both function1 and function2 in parallel? Imagine thread one (T-1) picks function1 to run and thread two (T-2) picks function2 to run. Now both threads are ready to run and here comes the problem. What if T-1 runs before T-2? Because both function1 and function2 depend on the global variable global, running these functions in parallel causes undesirable effects. Now change these functions into a pure function as explained in Listing 1-11.

Listing 1-11. Pure Functions

```
let function1 = (input,global) => {
        // works on input
        //changes global
        global = "somethingElse"
}
```

```
let function2 = (global) => {
        if(global === "something")
        {
                //business logic
        }
}
```

Here we have moved the global variable as arguments for both the functions, making them pure. Now we can run both functions in parallel without any issues. Because the functions don't depend on an external environment (global variable), we aren't worried about thread execution order as with Listing 1-10.

This section shows us how pure functions help our code to run in parallel without any problems.

Cachable

Because the pure function is going to always return the same output for the given input, we can cache the function outputs. To make this more concrete, we provide a simple example. Imagine we have a function that does time-consuming calculations. We name this function longRunningFunction:

```
var longRunningFunction = (ip) => { //do long running tasks and
return }
```

If the longRunningFunction function is a pure function, then we know that for the given input, it is going to return the same output. With that point in mind, why do we need to call the function again with its input multiple times? Can't we just replace the function call with the function's previous result? (Again note here how we are using the referential transparency concept, thus replacing the function with the previous result value and leaving the context unchanged.) Imagine we have a bookkeeping object that keeps all the function call results of longRunningFunction like this:

```
var longRunningFnBookKeeper = { 2 : 3, 4 : 5 . . .  }
```

The longRunningFnBookKeeper is a simple JavaScript object, which is going to hold all the input (as keys) and outputs (as values) in it as a result of invoking longRunningFunction functions. Now with our pure function definition in place, we can check if the key is present in longRunningFnBookKeeper before invoking our original function, as shown in Listing 1-12.

Listing 1-12. Caching Achieved via Pure Functions

```
var longRunningFnBookKeeper = { 2 : 3, 4 : 5 }
//check if the key present in longRunningFnBookKeeper
//if get back the result else update the bookkeeping object
longRunningFnBookKeeper.hasOwnProperty(ip) ?
        longRunningFnBookKeeper[ip] :
        longRunningFnBookKeeper[ip] = longRunningFunction(ip)
```

The code in Listing 1-12 is relatively straightforward. Before calling our real function, we are checking if the result of that function with the corresponding ip is in the bookkeeping object. If yes, we are returning it, or else we are calling our original function and updating the result in our bookkeeping object as well. Did you see how easily we have made the function calls cachable by using less code? That's the power of pure functions.

We will be writing a functional lib, which does the caching, or technical *memorization,* of our pure function calls later in the book.

Pipelines and Composable

With pure functions, we are going to do only one thing in that function. We have seen already how the pure function is going to act as a self-understanding of what that function does by seeing its name. Pure functions should be designed in such a way that they should do only one thing. Doing only one thing and doing it perfectly is a UNIX philosophy; we will be following the same while implementing our pure functions. There are many commands in UNIX and LINUX platforms that we are using for day-to-day tasks. For example, we use cat to print the contents of the file, grep to search the files, wc to count the lines, and so on. These commands do solve one problem at a time, but we can *compose* or *pipeline* to do the complex tasks. Imagine we want to find a specific name in a text file and count its occurrences. How will we be doing that in our command prompt? The command looks like this:

```
cat jsBook | grep -i "composing" | wc
```

This command does solve our problem via composing many functions. Composing is not only unique to UNIX/LINUX command lines; it is the heart of the functional programming paradigm. We call this *functional composition* in our world. Imagine these same command lines have been implemented in JavaScript functions. We can use them with the same principles to solve our problem.

Now think about another problem in a different way. You want to count the number of lines in text. How will you solve it? Ahaa! You got the answer. The commands are in fact a pure function with respect to our definition. It takes an argument and returns the output to the caller without affecting any of the external environments.

That's a lot of benefits we are getting by following a simple definition. Before we close this chapter, we want to show the relationship between a pure function and a mathematical function. We tackle that next.

A Pure Function Is a Mathematical Function

Earlier we saw this code snippet in Listing 1-12:

```
var longRunningFunction = (ip) => { //do long running tasks and
return }
var longRunningFnBookKeeper = { 2 : 3, 4 : 5 }
//check if the key present in longRunningFnBookKeeper
//if get back the result else update the bookkeeping object
longRunningFnBookKeeper.hasOwnProperty(ip) ?
        longRunningFnBookKeeper[ip] :
        longRunningFnBookKeeper[ip] = longRunningFunction(ip)
```

The primary aim was to cache the function calls. We did so using the bookkeeping object. Imagine we have called the longRunningFunction many times so that our longRunningFnBookKeeper grows into the object, which looks like this:

```
longRunningFnBookKeeper = {
    1 : 32,
    2 : 4,
    3 : 5,
    5 : 6,
    8 : 9,
    9 : 10,
    10 : 23,
    11 : 44
}
```

Now imagine that `longRunningFunction` input ranges only from 1 to 11 integers, for example. Because we have already built the bookkeeping object for this particular range, we can refer only the `longRunningFnBookKeeper` to say the output `longRunningFunction` for the given input.

Let's analyze this bookkeeping object. This object gives us the clear picture that our function `longRunningFunction` takes an input and *maps* over the output for the given range (in this case it's 1–11). The important point to note here is that the inputs (in this case, the keys) have, mandatorily, a corresponding output (in this case, the result) in the object. In addition, there is no input in the key section that maps to two outputs.

With this analysis we can revisit the mathematical function definition, this time providing a more concrete definition from Wikipedia (`https://en.wikipedia.org/wiki/Function_(mathematics)`):

> *In mathematics, a function is a relation between a set of inputs and a set of permissible outputs with the property that each input is related to exactly one output. The input to a function is called the argument and the output is called the value. The set of all permitted inputs to a given function is called the domain of the function, while the set of permissible outputs is called the codomain.*

This definition is exactly the same as our pure functions. Have a look at our `longRunningFnBookKeeper` object. Can you find the *domain* and *codomain* of our function? With this very simple example you can easily see how the mathematical function idea is borrowed in the functional paradigm world (as stated in the beginning of the chapter).

What We Are Going to Build

We have talked a lot about functions and functional programming in this chapter. With this fundamental knowledge we are going to build the functional library called ES8-Functional. This library will be built chapter by chapter throughout the text. By building the functional library you will be exploring how JavaScript functions can be used (in a functional way) and also how functional programming can be applied in day-to-day activities (using our created function to solve the problem in our code base).

Is JavaScript a Functional Programming Language?

Before we close this chapter, we have to take a step back and answer a fundamental question: Is JavaScript a functional programming language? The answer is yes and no. We said in the beginning of the chapter that functional programming is all about functions, which have to take at least an argument and return a value. To be frank, though, we can create a function in JavaScript that can take no argument and in fact return nothing. For example, the following code is a valid code in the JavaScript engine:

```
var useless = () => {}
```

This code will execute without any error in the JavaScript world. The reason is that JavaScript is not a pure functional language (like Haskell) but rather a multiparadigm language. However, the language is very much suitable for the functional programming paradigm as discussed in this chapter. The techniques and the benefits that we have discussed up to now can be applied in pure JavaScript. This is the reason for this book's title.

JavaScript is a language that has support for functions as arguments, passing functions to other functions, and so on, mainly because JavaScript treats functions as its first-class citizens (we talk more about this in upcoming chapters). Because of the constraints according to the definition of the term function, we as developers need to take them into account while creating them in the JavaScript world. By doing so, we will gain many advantages from the functional paradigm as discussed in this chapter.

Summary

In this chapter we have seen what functions are in math and in the programming world. We started with a simple definition of function in mathematics and reviewed small, solid examples of functions and the functional programming paradigm in JavaScript. We also defined what pure functions are and discussed, in detail, their benefits. At the end of the chapter we also showed the relationship between pure functions and mathematical functions. We also discussed how JavaScript could be treated as a functional programming language. A lot of progress has been made in this chapter.

In the next chapter, we will be reading about creating and executing functions in the ES8 context. Now with ES8 we have several ways to create functions; that's exactly what we will be reading about in the next chapter.

CHAPTER 2

Fundamentals of JavaScript Functions

In the previous chapter we saw what functional programming is all about. We saw how functions in the software world are nothing but mathematical functions. We spent a lot of time discussing how pure functions can bring us huge advantages such as parallel code execution, being cachable, and more. We are now convinced that functional programming is all about functions.

In this chapter we are going to see how functions in JavaScript can be used. We will be looking at the latest JavaScript version, ES7/8. This chapter is a refresher on how to create functions, call them, and pass arguments as defined in ES6 and later versions. That's not the goal of this book, though. We strongly recommend that you try all the code snippets in the book to get a gist of how to use functions (more precisely we will be working on *arrow functions*).

Once we have a solid understanding of how to use functions, we will be turning our focus to seeing how to run the ES8 code in our system. As of today, browsers don't support all features of ES8. To tackle that, we will be using a tool called *Babel*. At the end of the chapter we will be starting our groundwork for creating a functional library. For this purpose, we will be using a node project that will be set up using the Babel-Node tool to run our code in your system.

© Anto Aravinth, Srikanth Machiraju 2018
A. Aravinth and S. Machiraju, *Beginning Functional JavaScript*,
https://doi.org/10.1007/978-1-4842-4087-8_2

> **Note**   The chapter examples and library source code are in branch
> chap02. The repo's URL is `https://github.com/antsmartian/`
> `functional-es8.git`
>
> Once you check out the code, please check out branch chap02:
>
> ```
> ...
> git checkout -b chap02 origin/chap02
> ...
> ```
>
> For running the codes, as before run:
>
> ```
> ...
> npm run playground
> ...
> ```

ECMAScript: A Bit of History

ECMAScript is a specification of JavaScript, which is maintained by ECMA
International in ECMA-262 and ISO/IEC 16262. Here are the versions of
ECMAScript:

1. ECMAScript 1 was the very first version of the
   JavaScript language, released in 1997.

2. ECMAScript 2 is the second version of the JavaScript
   language, which contains very minor changes with
   respect to the previous version. This version was
   released in 1998.

3. ECMAScript 3 introduced several features and was
   released in 1999.

4. ECMAScript 5 is supported by almost all browsers today. This is the version that introduced *strict* mode into the language. It was released in 2009. ECMAScript 5.1 was released with minor corrections in June 2011.

5. ECMAScript 6 introduced many changes, including classes, symbols, arrow functions, generators, and so on.

6. ECMAScript 7 and 8 have new concepts like async await, SharedArrayBuffer, trailing commas, Object. entries, and so on.

We refer to ECMAScript as ES7 in this book, so these terms are interchangeable.

Creating and Executing Functions

In this section we are going to see how to create and execute functions in several ways in JavaScript. This section is going to be long and interesting as well. Because many browsers do not yet support ES6 or higher versions, we want to find a way to run our code smoothly. Meet *Babel,* a *transpiler* that can convert the latest code into valid ES5 code (note that in our history section, we mentioned ES5 code can be run in all browsers today). Converting the code into ES5 gives developers a way of seeing and using the features of the latest version of ECMAScript without any problem. Using Babel, we can run all the code samples that are presented in this book.

After you have installed Babel, we can get our hands dirty by seeing our first simple function.

First Function

We define our first simple function here. The simplest function one can write in ES6 or higher versions is given in Listing 2-1.

Listing 2-1. A Simple Function

```
() => "Simple Function"
```

If you try to run this function in babel-repl, you will see this result:

```
[Function]
```

Note   It's not necessary to run the code samples in the Babel world. If you're using the latest browser and you're sure that it supports the latest version of ECMAScript, then you can use your browser console to run the code snippets. After all it's a matter of choice. If you're running the code, say in Chrome, for example, Listing 2-1 should give you this result:

```
function () => "Simple Function"
```

The point to note here is the results might differ in showing the function *representation* based on where you're running the code snippets.

That's it: We have a function. Take a moment to analyze this function. Let's split them:

```
() => "Simple Function"

//where () represents function arguments
//=> starts the function body/definition
//content after => are the function body/definition.
```

We can skip the function keyword to define functions. You can see we have used the => operator to define the function body. Functions created this way are called *arrow functions.* We use arrow functions throughout the book.

Now that the function is defined, we can execute it to see the result. Oh wait, the function we have created doesn't have a name. How do we call it?

Note   Functions that don't have names are called anonymous functions. We will understand the usage of anonymous functions in the functional programming paradigm, when seeing higher order functions in Chapter 3.

Let's assign a name for it as shown in Listing 2-2.

Listing 2-2. A Simple Function with a Name

```
var simpleFn = () => "Simple Function"
```

Because we now have access to the function simpleFn we can use this reference to execute the function:

```
simpleFn()
//returns "Simple Function" in the console
```

Now we have created a function and also executed it. We can see how the same function looks alike in ES5. We can use babel to convert our code into ES5, using the following command:

```
babel simpleFn.js --presets babel-preset-es2015 --out-file
script-compiled.js
```

This will generate the file called `script-compiled.js` in your current directory. Now open the generated file in your favorite editor:

```
"use strict";

var simpleFn = function simpleFn() {
  return "Simple Function";
};
```

That's our equivalent code in ES5. You can sense how it is much easier and more concise to write functions in the latest versions. There are two important points to note in the converted code snippets. We discuss them one after the other.

Strict Mode

In this section we discuss strict mode in JavaScript. We'll see its benefits and why one should prefer strict mode.

You can see that the converted code runs in `strict` mode, as shown here:

```
"use strict";

var simpleFn = function simpleFn() {
  return "Simple Function";
};
```

Strict mode has nothing to do with the latest versions, but discussing it here is appropriate. As we have already discussed, strict mode was introduced to JavaScript language with ES5.

Simply put, strict mode is a restricted variant of JavaScript. The same JavaScript code that is running in strict mode can be semantically different from the code, which is not using strict mode. All the code snippets that don't use strict in their JavaScript files are going to be in nonstrict mode.

Why should we use strict mode? What are the advantages? There are many advantages of using strict mode style in the world of JavaScript. One simple advantage occurs if you are defining a variable in global state (i.e., without specifying var command) like this:

`"use strict";`

```
globalVar = "evil"
```

In strict mode it's going to be an error! That's a good catch for our developers, because global variables are very evil in JavaScript. However, if the same code were run in nonstrict mode, then it wouldn't have complained about the error.

Now as you can guess, the same code in JavaScript can produce different results whether you're running in strict or nonstrict mode. Because strict mode is going to be very helpful for us, we will leave Babel to use strict mode while transpiling our ES8 codes.

Note   We can place use stricts in the beginning of a JavaScript file, in which case it's going to apply its check for the full functions defined in the particular file. Otherwise, you can use strict mode only for specific functions. In that case, strict mode will be applied only to that particular function, leaving other function behaviors in nonstrict mode. For more information on this, see `https://developer.mozilla.org/en-US/docs/Web/JavaScript/Reference/Strict_mode`.

Return Statement Is Optional

In the ES5 converted code snippet, we saw that Babel adds the `return` statement in our `simpleFn`.

```
"use strict";

var simpleFn = function simpleFn() {
  return "Simple Function";
};
```

In our real code, though, we didn't specify any `return` statement:

```
var simpleFn = () => "Simple Function"
```

Thus here, if you have a function with only a single statement then it implicitly means that it returns the value. What about multiple statement functions? How we are going to create them?

Multiple Statement Functions

Now we are going to see how to write multiple statement functions. Let's make our `simpleFn` a bit more complicated, as shown in Listing 2-3.

Listing 2-3. Multistatement Function

```
var simpleFn = () => {
   let value = "Simple Function"
   return value;
} //for multiple statement wrap with { }
```

Run this function, and you will get the same result as before. Here, though, we have used multiple arguments to achieve the same behavior. Apart from that, notice that we have used the `let` keyword to define our `value` variable. The `let` keyword is new to the JavaScript keyword family.

It allows you to declare variables that are limited to a particular scope of block, unlike the var keyword, which defines the variable globally to a function regardless of the block in which it is defined.

To make the point concrete, we can write the same function with var and the let keyword, inside an if block as shown in Listing 2-4.

Listing 2-4. SimpleFn with var and let Keywords

```
var simpleFn = () => { //function scope
    if(true) {
        let a = 1;
        var b = 2;
        console.log(a)
        console.log(b)
    } //if block scope
    console.log(b) //function scope
    console.log(a) //function scope
}
```

Running this function gives the following output:

```
1
2
2
Uncaught ReferenceError: a is not defined(...)
```

As you can see from the output, the variable declared via the let keyword is accessible only within the if block, not outside the block. JavaScript throws the error when we access a variable outside the block, whereas the variable declared with var doesn't act that way. Rather, it declares the variable scope for the whole function. That's the reason variable b can be accessed outside the if block.

Because block scope is very much needed going forward, we will be using the let keyword for defining variables throughout the book. Now let's see how to create a function with arguments as the final section.

Function Arguments

Creating functions with arguments is the same as in ES5. Look at a quick example as follows (Listing 2-5).

Listing 2-5. Function with Argument

```
let identity = (value) => value
```

Here we create a function called identity, which takes value as its argument and returns the same. As you can see, creating functions with arguments is the same as in ES5; only the syntax of creating the function is changed.

ES5 Functions Are Valid in ES6 and Above

Before we close this section, we need to make an important point clear. The functions that were written in ES5 are still valid in the latest version(s). It's just a small matter that newer versions have introduced arrow functions, but that doesn't replace the old function syntax or anything else. However, we will be using arrow functions throughout this book to showcase the functional programming approach.

Setting Up Our Project

Now that we understand how to create arrow functions, we shift our focus to project setup in this section. We are going to set up our project as a node project and at the end of the section, we will be writing our first functional function.

Initial Setup

In this section, we follow a simple step-by-step guide to set up our environment. The steps are as follows.

1. The first step is to create a directory where our source code is going to be. Create a directory and name it whatever you want.

2. Go into that particular directory and run the following command from your terminal:

   ```
   npm init
   ```

3. After running Step 2, you will be asked a set of questions; you can provide the value you want. Once it's done, it will create a file called package. json in your current directory.

The project package.json that we have created looks like Listing 2-6.

Listing 2-6. Package.json Contents

```json
{
  "name": "learning-functional",
  "version": "1.0.0",
  "description": "Functional lib and examples in ES8",
  "main": "index.js",
  "scripts": {
    "test": "echo \"Error: no test specified\" && exit 1"
  },
  "author": "Anto Aravinth @antoaravinth",
  "license": "ISC"
}
```

Now we need to add a few libraries, which will allow us to write ES8 code and execute them. Run the following command in the current directory:

```
npm install --save-dev babel-preset-es2017-node7
```

Note   The book uses Babel version "babel-preset-es2017-node7." This specific version might be outdated by the time you read this text. You are free to install the latest version, and everything should work smoothly. However, in the context of the book, we will be using the specified version.

This command downloads the babel package called ES2017; the main aim of this package is to allow the latest ECMAScript code to run on the Node Js platform. The reason is that Node Js, at the time of writing this book, is not fully compatible with the latest features.

Once this command is run, you will be able to see a folder called node_modules created in the directory, which has the babel-preset-es2017 folder.

Because we have used --save-dev while installing, npm does add the corresponding babel dependencies to our package.json. Now if you open your package.json, it looks like Listing 2-7.

Listing 2-7. After Adding devDependencies

```
{
  "name": "learning-functional",
  "version": "1.0.0",
  "description": "Functional lib and examples",
  "main": "index.js",
  "scripts": {
    "test": "echo \"Error: no test specified\" && exit 1"
  },
```

```
"author": "Anto Aravinth @antoaravinth>",
"license": "ISC",
"devDependencies": {
  "babel-preset-es2017-node7": "^0.5.2",
  "babel-cli": "^6.23.0"
}
}
```

Now that this is in place, we can go ahead and create two directories called lib and functional-playground. So now your directory looks like this:

```
learning-functional
  - functional-playground
  - lib
  - node_modules
    - babel-preset-es2017-node7/*
  - package.json
```

Now we are going to put all our functional library code into lib and use functional-playground to explore and understand our functional techniques.

Our First Functional Approach to the Loop Problem

Imagine we have to iterate through the array and print the data to the console. How do we achieve this in JavaScript?

Listing 2-8. Looping an Array

```
var array = [1,2,3]
for(i=0;i<array.length;i++)
    console.log(array[i])
```

As we have already discussed in Chapter 1, abstracting the operations into functions is one of the pillars of functional programming. Let's abstract this operation into function, so that we can reuse it any time we need to rather than repeating ourselves in telling it how to iterate the loop.

Create a file called es8-functional.js in the lib directory. Our directory structure looks like this:

```
learning-functional
    - functional-playground
    - lib
      - es8-functional.js
    - node_modules
      - babel-preset-es2017-node7/*
    - package.json
```

Now with that file in place, go ahead and place the content of Listing 2-9 into that file.

Listing 2-9. forEach Function

```
const forEach = (array,fn) => {
    let i;
    for(i=0;i<array.length;i++)
      fn(array[i])
}
```

Note   For now don't worry about how this function works. We are going to see how higher order functions work in JavaScript in the next chapter and provide loads of examples.

You might notice that we have started with a keyword const for our function definition. This keyword is part of the latest version, which makes the declaration constant. For example, if someone tries to reassign the variable with the same name like this:

```
forEach = "" //making your function as string!
```

The preceding code will throw an error like this:

```
TypeError: Assignment to constant variable.
```

This will prevent it from being accidentally reassigned. Now we'll go and use the created function to print all the data of the array to the console. To do that, create a file called play.js function in the functional-playground directory. So now the current file looks like this:

```
learning-functional
  - functional-playground
    - play.js
  - lib
    - es8-functional.js
  - node_modules
    - babel-preset-es2017-node7/*
  - package.json
```

We will call the forEach in our play.js file. How are we are going to call this function, which resides in a different file?

Gist on Exports

ES6 also introduced the concept called *modules*. ES6 modules are stored in files. In our case we can think of the es8-functional.js file itself as a module. Along with the concept of modules came import and export statements. In our running example, we have to *export* the forEach function so that others can use it. We can add the code shown in Listing 2-10 to our es8-functional.js file.

Listing 2-10. Exporting forEach Function

```
const forEach = (array,fn) => {
   let i;
   for(i=0;i<array.length;i++)
      fn(array[i])
}
export default forEach
```

Gist on Imports

Now that we have exported our function as you can see in Listing 2-10, let's go and consume it via import. Open the file play.js and add the code shown in Listing 2-11.

Listing 2-11. Importing forEach Function

```
import forEach from '../lib/es8-functional.js'
```

This line tells JavaScript to import the function called forEach from es8-functional.js. Now the function is available to the whole file with the name forEach. Now add the code into play.js as shown in Listing 2-12.

Listing 2-12. Using the Imported forEach Function

```
import forEach from '../lib/es8-functional.js'
var array = [1,2,3]
forEach(array,(data) => console.log(data)) //refereing to
imported forEach
```

Running the Code Using Babel-Node

Let's run our play.js file. Because we are using the latest version in our file, we have to use Babel-Node to run our code. Babel-Node is used to transpile our code and run it on Node js. Babel-Node should be installed along with babel-cli.

So, from our project root directory, we can call the babel-node like this:

```
babel-node functional-playground/play.js --presets es2017
```

This command tells us that our play.js file should be transpiled with es2017 and run into node js. This should give the output as follows:

```
1
2
3
```

Hurray! Now we have abstracted out for logic into a function. Imagine you want to iterate and print the array contents with multiples of 2. How will we do it? Simply reuse our forEach, which will print the output as expected:

```
forEach(array,(data) => console.log(2 * data))
```

Note   We will be using this pattern throughout the book. We discuss the problem with an imperative approach and then go ahead and implement our functional techniques and capture them in a function into es8-functional.js. We then use that to play around in the play.js file!

Creating Script in Npm

We have seen how to run our play.js file, but it's a lot to type. Each time we need to run the following:

```
babel-node functional-playground/play.js --presets es2015-node5
```

Rather than entering this, we can bind the command shown in Listing 2-13 to our npm script. We will change the package.json accordingly:

Listing 2-13. Adding npm Scripts to package.json

```
{
  "name": "learning-functional",
  "version": "1.0.0",
  "description": "Functional lib and examples",
  "main": "index.js",
  "scripts": {
    "playground" : "babel-node functional-playground/play.js
    --presets es2017-node7"
  },
  "author": "Anto Aravinth @antoaravinth",
  "license": "ISC",
```

```
"devDependencies": {
  "babel-preset-es2017-node7": "^0.5.2"
}
}
```

Now we have added the babel-node command to scripts, so we can run our playground file (node `functional-playground/play.js`) as follows:

```
npm run playground
```

This will run the same as before.

Running the Source Code from Git

Whatever we are discussing in the chapter will go into a git repository (`https://github.com/antoaravinth/functional-es8`). You can clone them into your system using git like this:

```
git clone https://github.com/antsmartian/functional-es8.git
```

Once you clone the repo, you can move into a specific chapter source code branch. Each chapter has its own branch in the repo. For example, to see the code samples used in Chapter 2, you need to enter this:

```
git checkout -b chap02 origin/chap02
```

Once you check out the branch, you can run the playground file as before.

Summary

In this chapter, we have spent a lot of time learning how to use functions. We have taken advantage of Babel tools for running our code seamlessly in our Node platform. We also created our project as a node project. In our node project, we saw how to use Babel-node to convert the code and run them in a node environment using presets. We also saw how to download the book source code and run it. With all these techniques under our belt, in the next chapter we will be focusing on what higher order functions mean. We will explain the Async/Await features of ES7 in later chapters.

CHAPTER 3

Higher Order Functions

In the previous chapter we saw how to create simple functions in ES8. We also set up our environment to play around with functional programs using a node ecosystem. In fact, we created our first functional program application programming interface (API) called forEach in the previous chapter. There is something special about the forEach function that we developed in Chapter 2. We passed a function itself as an argument to our forEach function. There is no trick involved there; it's part of the JavaScript specification that a function can be passed as an argument. JavaScript as a language treats functions as data. This is a very powerful concept that allows us to pass functions in place of data. A function that takes another function as its argument is called a higher order function.

We are going to see higher order functions (HOC for short) in this chapter in depth. We start the chapter with a simple example and definition of HOC. Later we provide more real-world examples of how HOC can help a programmer to solve complex problems easily. As before, we will be adding the HOC functions that we are creating in the chapter to our library. Let's get started!

We will be creating a few higher order functions and adding them to our library. We are doing this to show how things work behind the scenes. The library is good for learning current resources, but they are not production ready for the library, so keep that in mind.

© Anto Aravinth, Srikanth Machiraju 2018
A. Aravinth and S. Machiraju, *Beginning Functional JavaScript*,
https://doi.org/10.1007/978-1-4842-4087-8_3

> **Note**   The chapter examples and library source code are in branch
> chap03. The repo's URL is: `https://github.com/antsmartian/`
> `functional-es8.git`
>
> Once you check out the code, please check out branch chap03:
>
> ```
> ...
> git checkout -b chap03 origin/chap03
> ...
> ```
>
> For running the codes, as before run:
>
> ```
> ...
> npm run playground
> ...
> ```

Understanding Data

As programmers, we know our programs act on *data*. Data is something
that is very important for the consumption of our written program to
execute. Hence almost all programming languages give several data for
the programmer to work with. For example, we can store the name of a
person in the String data type. JavaScript offers several data types that we
cover in the next subsection. At the end of the section, we introduce a solid
definition of higher order functions, with simple and concise examples.

Understanding JavaScript Data Types

Every programming language has data types. These data types can hold
data and allow our program to act on it. In this brief section, we introduce
JavaScript data types.

In a nutshell, JavaScript as a language supports the following data types:

- Numbers
- Strings
- Booleans
- Objects
- null
- undefined

Importantly, we also have our friend `functions` as a data type in JavaScript language. Because `functions` are data types like `String`, we can pass them around, store them in a variable, and so on. Functions are first-class citizens when the language permits them to be used as any other data type; that is, functions can be assigned to variables, passed around as arguments, and returned from other functions similarly as we do for `String` and `Numbers` data. In the next section we provide a quick example of what we mean by storing and passing functions around.

Storing a Function

As previously mentioned, `functions` are nothing but data. Because they are data, we can hold them in a variable! The code in Listing 3-1 is valid code in a JavaScript context.

Listing 3-1. Storing a Function in Variable

```
let fn = () => {}
```

In this code snippet, fn is nothing but a variable that is pointing to a data type function. We can quickly check that fn is of type function by running the following code:

```
typeof fn
=> "function"
```

Because fn is just a reference to our function, we can call it like this:

```
fn()
```

This will execute the function that fn points to.

Passing a Function

As day-to-day JavaScript programmers, we know how to pass data to a function. Consider the following function (Listing 3-2), which takes an argument and logs to console the type of the argument:

Listing 3-2. tellType Function

```
let tellType = (arg) => {
        console.log(typeof arg)
}
```

One can pass the argument to the tellType function to see it in action:

```
let data = 1
tellType(data)
=> number
```

There is nothing fancy here. As seen in the previous section, we can store even functions in our variable (as functions in JavaScript are data). So how about passing a variable that has reference to a function? Let's quickly check it:

```
let dataFn = () => {
        console.log("I'm a function")
}
tellType(dataFn)
=> function
```

That's great! Now we will make our `tellType` execute the passed argument as shown in Listing 3-3 if it is of type `function`:

Listing 3-3. `tellType` Executes `arg` if It Is a Function

```
var tellType = (arg) => {
   if(typeof arg === "function")
      arg()
   else
          console.log("The passed data is " + arg)
}
```

Here we are checking whether the passed `arg` is of type `function`; if so, call it. Remember if a variable is of type `function`, it means it has a reference to a function that can be executed. That is the reason we are calling `arg()` if it enters an `if` statement in the code in Listing 3-3.

Let's execute our `tellType` function by passing our `dataFn` variable to it:

```
tellType(dataFn)
=> I'm a function
```

We have successfully passed a function `dataFn` to another function `tellType`, which has executed the passed function. It is that simple.

Returning a Function

We have seen how to pass a function to another function. Because functions are simple data in JavaScript, we can return them from other functions, too (like other data types).

We'll take a simple example of a function that returns another function as shown in Listing 3-4.

Listing 3-4. Crazy Function Return String

```
let crazy = () => { return String }
```

Note   JavaScript has a built-in function called String. We can use this function to create new string values in JavaScript like this:

```
String("HOC")
=> HOC
```

Note that our crazy function returns a function reference that is pointing to String function. Let's call our crazy function:

```
crazy()
=> String() { [native code] }
```

As you can see, calling the crazy function returns a String function. Note that it just returns the function reference and does not execute the function. We can hold back the returned function reference and call them like this:

```
let fn = crazy()
fn("HOC")
=> HOC
```

or even better like this:

```
crazy()("HOC")
=> HOC
```

Note   We use simple documentation on top of all functions that are going to return another function. It will be really helpful going forward as it makes reading the source code easy. For example, the `crazy` function will be documented like this:

```
//Fn => String
```

```
let crazy = () => { return String }
```

The `Fn => String` comment helps the reader understand that `crazy` function, which executes and returns another function that points to `String`.

We use these sorts of readable comments in this book.

In these sections we have seen functions that take other functions as their argument and have also seen examples of functions that do not return another function. Now it's time to bring you to the definition of a higher order function: a function that receives the function as its argument, returns it as output, or both.

Abstraction and Higher Order Functions

We have seen how to create and execute higher order functions. Generally speaking, higher order functions are usually written to abstract common problems. In other words, higher order functions are nothing but defining *abstractions*.

In this section we discuss the relationship that higher order functions have with the term *abstraction*.

Abstraction Definitions

Wikipedia helps us by providing this definition of abstraction:

> In software engineering and computer science, abstraction is a technique for managing complexity of computer systems. It works by establishing a level of complexity on which a person interacts with the system, suppressing the more complex details below the current level. The programmer works with an idealized interface (usually well defined) and can add additional levels of functionality that would otherwise be too complex to handle.

It also includes the following text, which is what we are interested in:

> For example, a programmer writing code that involves numerical operations may not be interested in the way numbers are represented in the underlying hardware (e.g., whether they're 16 bit or 32 bit integers), and where those details have been suppressed it can be said that they were *abstracted away*, leaving simply numbers with which the programmer can work.

This text clearly gives the idea of abstraction. Abstraction allows us to work on the desired goal without worrying about the underlying system concepts.

Abstraction via Higher Order Functions

In this section we will see how higher order functions help us to achieve the abstraction concept we discussed in the previous section. Here is the code snippet of our forEach function defined in Chapter 2 (Listing 2-9):

```
const forEach = (array,fn) => {
        for(let i=0;array.length;i++)
                fn(array[i])
}
```

The preceding forEach function here has abstracted away the problem of traversing the array. The user of the forEach API does not need to understand how forEach has implemented the traversing part, thus abstracting away the problem.

Note   In the forEach function, the passed function fn is called with a single argument as the current iteration content of the array, as you can see here:

• • •

fn(array[i])

• • •

So when the user of the forEach function calls it like this:

```
forEach([1,2,3],(data) => {
//data is passed from forEach function
//to this current function as argument
})
```

---

forEach essentially traverses the array. What about traversing a JavaScript object? Traversing a JavaScript object has steps like this:

1. Iterate all the keys of the given object.

2. Identify that the key belongs to its own object.

3. Get the value of the key if Step 2 is true.

Let's abstract these steps into a higher order function named forEachObject, as shown in Listing 3-5.

Listing 3-5. forEachObject Function Definition

```
const forEachObject = (obj,fn) => {
    for (var property in obj) {
            if (obj.hasOwnProperty(property)) {
                //calls the fn with key and value as its argument
                fn(property, obj[property])
            }
    }
}
```

Note   forEachObject takes the first argument as a JavaScript object (as obj) and the second argument is a function fn. It traverses the object using the precedng algorithm and calls the fn with key and value as its argument, respectively.

Here they are in action:

```
let object = {a:1,b:2}
forEachObject(object, (k,v) => console.log(k + ":" + v))
=> a:1
=> b:1
```

Cool! An important point to note is that both forEach and forEachObject functions are higher order functions, which allow the developer to work on task (by passing the corresponding function), abstracting away the traversing part! Because these traversing functions are being abstracted away, we can test them thoroughly, leading to a concise code base. Let's implement an abstracted way for handling control flows.

For that, let us create a function called unless. Unless is a simple function that takes a predicate (which should be either true or false); if the predicate is false, call the fn as shown in Listing 3-6.

Listing 3-6. unless Function Definition

```
const unless = (predicate,fn) => {
        if(!predicate)
                fn()
}
```

With the unless function in place, we can write a concise piece of code to find the list of even numbers. The code for it looks like this:

```
forEach([1,2,3,4,5,6,7],(number) => {
        unless((number % 2), () => {
                console.log(number, " is even")
        })
})
```

This code, when executed, is going to print the following:

```
2 ' is even'
4 ' is even'
6 ' is even'
```

In this case we are getting the even numbers from the array list. What if we want to get the list of even numbers from, say, 0 to 100? We cannot use forEach here (of course we can, if we have the array that has [0,1,2....,100] content). Let's meet another higher order function called times. Times is yet another simple higher order function that takes the number and calls the passed function as many times as the caller indicates. The times function is shown in Listing 3-7.

Listing 3-7. times Function Definition

```
const times = (times, fn) => {
  for (var i = 0; i < times; i++)
      fn(i);
}
```

The times function looks very similar to the forEach function; it's just that we are operating on a Number rather than an Array. Now with the times function in place, we can go ahead and solve our problem at hand like this:

```
times(100, function(n) {
  unless(n % 2, function() {
    console.log(n, "is even");
  });
});
```

That's going to print our expected answer:

```
0 'is even'
2 'is even'
4 'is even'
6 'is even'
8 'is even'
10 'is even'
. . .

. . .
94 'is even'
96 'is even'
98 'is even'
```

With this code we have abstracted away looping, and the condition checks into a simple and concise higher order function!

Having seen a few examples of higher order functions, it's time to go one step further. In the upcoming section, we will discuss real-world higher order functions and how to create them.

Note   All the higher order functions that we are creating in this chapter will be in the chap03 branch.

Higher Order Functions in the Real World

In this section we will introduce real-world examples of higher order functions. We are going to start with simple higher order functions and slowly move into more complex higher order functions, which are used by JavaScript developers in their day-to-day lives. Excited? So what are you waiting for? Read on.

Note   The examples are continued in the next chapters after we introduce the concept of *closures*. Most of the higher order functions work with the help of closures.

---

every Function

Often JavaScript developers need to check if the array of content is a number, custom object, or anything else. We usually use a typical for loop approach to solve these problems, but let's abstract these away into a function called every. The every function takes two arguments: an array and a function. It checks if all the elements of the array are evaluated to true by the passed function. The implementation looks like Listing 3-8:

Listing 3-8. every Function Definition

```
const every = (arr,fn) => {
    let result = true;
    for(let i=0;i<arr.length;i++)
        result = result && fn(arr[i])
    return result
}
```

Here we are simply iterating over the passed array and calling the fn by passing the current content of the array element at the iteration. Note that the passed fn should be returning a Boolean value. Then we use && to make sure all the contents of the array are obeying the criteria that are given by the fn.

We need to quickly check that our **every** function works fine. Then pass on the array of NaN and pass fn as isNaN, which does check if the given number is NaN or not:

```
every([NaN, NaN, NaN], isNaN)
=> true
every([NaN, NaN, 4], isNaN)
=> false
```

Great. The every is a typical higher order function that is easy to implement and it's very useful too! Before we go further, we need to make ourselves comfortable with the for..of loop. For..of loops can be used to iterate the array elements. Let's rewrite our **every** function with a for loop (Listing 3-9).

Listing 3-9. every Function with for..of Loop

```
const every = (arr,fn) => {
    let result = true;
    for(const value of arr)
```

```
        result = result && fn(value)
    return result
}
```

The `for..of` loop is just an abstraction over our old `for` loop. As you can see here, the `for..of` has eliminated the traversing of an array by hiding the index variable, and so on. We have abstracted away `for..of` with `every`. It's all about abstraction. What if the next version of JavaScript changes the way of `for..of`? We just need to change it in the `every` function. This is one of the most important advantages of abstraction.

some Function

Similar to the `every` function, we also have a function called `some`. The `some` works quite the opposite way of the `every` function such that the `some` function returns `true` if either one of the elements in the array returns `true` for the passed function. The `some` function is also called as **any** function. To implement the `some` function we use `||` rather than `&&`, as shown in Listing 3-10.

Listing 3-10. some Function Definition

```
const some = (arr,fn) => {
    let result = false;
    for(const value of arr)
        result = result || fn(value)
    return result
}
```

Note   Both every and some functions are inefficient implementations for large arrays as the every function should traverse the array until the first element that doesn't match the criteria, and the some function should traverse the array only until the first match. Remember that we are trying to understand the concepts of higher order functions in this chapter rather than writing code for efficiency and accuracy.

With the some function in place, we can check its result by passing the arrays like this:

```
some([NaN,NaN, 4], isNaN)
=>true
some([3,4, 4], isNaN)
=>false
```

Having seen both some and every function, let's look at the sort function and how a higher order function plays an important role there.

sort Function

The sort is a built-in function that is available in the Array prototype of JavaScript. Suppose we need to sort a list of fruits:

```
var fruit = ['cherries', 'apples', 'bananas'];
```

You can simply call the sort function that is available on the Array prototype:

```
fruit.sort()
=> ["apples", "bananas", "cherries"]
```

That's so simple. The sort function is a higher order function that takes up a function as its argument, which will help the sort function to decide the sorting logic. Simply put, the signature of the sort function looks like this:

```
arr.sort([compareFunction])
```

Here the compareFunction is optional. If the compareFunction is not supplied, elements are sorted by converting them to strings and comparing strings in Unicode code point order. You don't need to worry about Unicode conversion in this section as we are more focused on the higher order functions. The important point to note here is that to compare the element with our own logic while sorting is performed, we need to pass our compareFunction. We can sense how the sort function is designed to be so flexible in such a way that it can sort any data in the JavaScript world, provided we pass a compareFunction. The sort function is flexible due to the nature of higher order functions!

Before writing our compareFunction, let's see what it should really implement. The compareFunction should implement the logic shown in Listing 3-11 as mentioned at https://developer.mozilla.org/en-US/docs/Web/JavaScript/Reference/Global_Objects/Array/sort.

Listing 3-11. Skeleton of compare Function

```
function compare(a, b) {
  if (a is less than b by some ordering criterion) {
    return -1;
  }
  if (a is greater than b by the ordering criterion) {
    return 1;
  }
  // a must be equal to b
  return 0;
}
```

As a simple example, imagine we have a list of people:

```
var people = [
    {firstname: "aaFirstName", lastname: "cclastName"},
    {firstname: "ccFirstName", lastname: "aalastName"},
    {firstname:"bbFirstName", lastname:"bblastName"}
];
```

Now we need to sort people using the firstname key in the object, then we need to pass on our own compareFunction like this:

```
people.sort((a,b) => { return (a.firstname < b.firstname) ? -1 :
(a.firstname > b.firstname) ? 1 : 0 })
```

which is going to return the following data:

```
[ { firstname: 'aaFirstName', lastname: 'cclastName' },
  { firstname: 'bbFirstName', lastname: 'bblastName' },
  { firstname: 'ccFirstName', lastname: 'aalastName' } ]
```

Sorting with respect to lastname looks like this:

```
people.sort((a,b) => { return (a.lastname < b.lastname) ? -1 :
(a.lastname > b.lastname) ? 1 : 0 })
```

will return:

```
[ { firstname: 'ccFirstName', lastname: 'aalastName' },
  { firstname: 'bbFirstName', lastname: 'bblastName' },
  { firstname: 'aaFirstName', lastname: 'cclastName' } ]
```

Hooking again into the logic of compareFunction:

```
function compare(a, b) {
  if (a is less than b by some ordering criterion) {
    return -1;
  }
```

```
if (a is greater than b by the ordering criterion) {
  return 1;
}
// a must be equal to b
return 0;
}
```

Having known the algorithm for our compareFunction, can we do it better? Rather than writing the compareFunction every time, can we abstract away this logic into a function? As you can see in the preceding example, we wrote two functions each for comparing firstName and lastName with almost the same duplicate code. Let's solve this problem with our higher order function. Now the function that we are going to design won't take a function as its argument but rather return a function. (Remember HOC can also return a function.)

Let's call this function sortBy, which allows the user to sort the array of objects based on the passed property as shown in Listing 3-12.

Listing 3-12. sortBy Function Definition

```
const sortBy = (property) => {
    return (a,b) => {
        var result = (a[property] < b[property]) ? -1 :
        (a[property] > b[property]) ? 1 : 0;
        return result;
    }
}
```

The sortBy function takes an argument named property and returns a new function that takes two arguments:

. . .

```
    return (a,b) => { }
```

. . .

The returned function has a very simple function body that clearly shows the compareFunction logic:

```
. . .
(a[property] < b[property]) ? -1 : (a[property] > b[property])
? 1 : 0;
. . .
```

Imagine we are going to call the function with the property name firstname, and then the function body with the replaced property argument looks like this:

```
(a,b) => return (a['firstname'] < b['firstname']) ? -1 :
(a['firstname'] > b['firstname']) ? 1 : 0;
```

That's exactly what we did by manually writing a function. Here is our sortBy function in action:

```
people.sort(sortBy("firstname"))
```

will return:

```
[ { firstname: 'aaFirstName', lastname: 'cclastName' },
  { firstname: 'bbFirstName', lastname: 'bblastName' },
  { firstname: 'ccFirstName', lastname: 'aalastName' } ]
```

Sorting with respect to lastname looks like this:

```
people.sort(sortBy("lastname"))
```

returns:

```
[ { firstname: 'ccFirstName', lastname: 'aalastName' },
  { firstname: 'bbFirstName', lastname: 'bblastName' },
  { firstname: 'aaFirstName', lastname: 'cclastName' } ]
```

as before. Wow, that's truly amazing! The `sort` function takes the `compareFunction`, which is returned by the `sortBy` function! That's a lot of higher order functions floating around! Again we have abstracted away the logic behind `compareFunction`, leaving the user to focus on what he or she really needs. After all, a higher order function is all about abstractions.

Pause for a moment here, though, and think about the `sortBy` function. Remember that our `sortBy` function takes a property and returns another function. The returned function is what passed as `compareFunction` to our `sort` function. The question here is why the returned function carries the `property` argument value that we have passed.

Welcome to the world of closures! The `sortBy` function works just because JavaScript supports closures. We need to clearly understand what closures are before we go ahead and write higher order functions. Closures are the topic of the next chapter.

Remember, though, that we will be writing our real-world higher order function after explaining closures in the next chapter!

Summary

We started with simple data types that JavaScript supports. We found that `function` is also a data type in JavaScript. Thus, we can keep functions in all the places where we can keep our data. In other words, `function` can be stored, passed, and reassigned like other data types in JavaScript. This extreme feature of JavaScript allows the `function` to be passed over to another function, which we call a higher order function. Remember that a higher order function is a function that takes another function as its argument or returns a function. We saw a handful of examples in this chapter showcasing how these higher order function concepts help developers to write code that abstracts away the difficult part! We have created and added a few such functions in our own library. We concluded the chapter by mentioning that higher order functions work with the blessing of another important concept in JavaScript called closures, which are the topic of Chapter 4.

CHAPTER 4

Closures and Higher Order Functions

In the previous chapter we saw how higher order functions help developers create abstraction over common problems. It's a very powerful concept, as we learned. We have created our sortBy higher order function to showcase a valid and relevant example of the use case. Even though the sortBy function is working on the basis of higher order functions (which is again the concept of passing functions as arguments to the other functions), it has something to do with yet another concept called closures in JavaScript.

We need to understand closures in the JavaScript world before we go further in our journey of functional programming techniques. That's where this chapter comes into the picture. In this chapter we are going to discuss in detail what is meant by closures and at the same time continue our journey of writing useful and real-world higher order functions. The concept of closures has to do with scopes in JavaScript, so let's get started with closures in the next section.

© Anto Aravinth, Srikanth Machiraju 2018
A. Aravinth and S. Machiraju, *Beginning Functional JavaScript*,
https://doi.org/10.1007/978-1-4842-4087-8_4

Note   The chapter examples and library source code are in branch chap04. The repo's URL is https://github.com/ antoaravinth/functional-es8.git

Once you check out the code, please check out branch chap04:

```
...
git checkout -b chap04 origin/chap04
...
```

For running the codes, as before run:

```
...
npm run playground
...
```

Understanding Closures

In this section we are going to explain what we mean by closures with a simple example and then move on to our sortBy function by unwrapping how it works with closures.

What Are Closures?

Simply put, a closure is an inner function. So what is an inner function? It is just a function within another function, something like the following:

```
function outer() {
    function inner() {
    }
}
```

Yes, that's exactly what a closure is. The function inner is called a *closure function*. Closure is powerful because of its access to the scope chains (or scope levels). We will discuss scope chains in this section.

Note   Scope chains and scope levels mean the same, so they are used interchangeably in this chapter.

Technically the closure has access to three scopes:

1.   Variables that are declared in its own declaration.

2.   Access to the global variables.

3.   Access to the outer function's variable (interesting).

Let's talk about these three points separately with a simple example. Consider the following code snippet:

```
function outer() {
    function inner() {
        let a = 5;
        console.log(a)
    }
    inner() //call the inner function.
}
```

What will be printed to the console when the inner function gets called? The value will be 5. This is mainly due to the first point. A closure function can access all the variables declared in its own declaration (see Point 1). No rocket science here!

Note   A strong takeaway from the preceding code snippet is that the inner function won't be visible outside the outer function! Go ahead and test it.

Now modify the preceding code snippet to the following:

```
let global = "global"
function outer() {
    function inner() {
        let a = 5;
        console.log(global)
    }
    inner() //call the inner function.
}
```

Now when the `inner` function is executed, it does print the value global. Thus closures can access the global variable (see Point 2).

Points 1 and 2 are now clear with the example. The third point is very interesting, and the claim can be seen in the following code:

```
let global = "global"
function outer() {
    let outer = "outer"
    function inner() {
        let a = 5;
        console.log(outer)
    }
    inner() //call the inner function.
}
```

Now when the `inner` function executes, it does print the value outer. This looks reasonable, but it is a very important property of a closure. Closure has access to the outer function's variable(s). Here outer function means the function that encloses the closure function. This property is what makes the closures so powerful!

Note   Closure also has access to the enclosing function parameters. Try adding a paramater to our `outer` function and try to access it from the `inner` function. We will wait here until you are done with this small exercise.

Remembering Where It Is Born

In the previous section we saw what a closure is. Now we will be seeing a slightly complicated example, which explains yet another important concept in closure: closure remembering its context.

Take a look at the following code:

```
var fn = (arg) => {
        let outer = "Visible"
        let innerFn = () => {
                console.log(outer)
                console.log(arg)
        }
        return innerFn
}
```

The code is simple. The `innerFn` is a closure function to `fn` and `fn` returns the `innerFn` when called. There is nothing fancy here.

Let's play around with `fn`:

```
var closureFn = fn(5);
closureFn()
```

will print the following:

```
Visible
5
```

How does calling `closureFn` print `Visible` and `5` to the console? What is happening behind the scenes? Let's break it down.

There are two steps happening in this case:

1. When this line is called:

   ```
   var closureFn = fn(5);
   ```

   our `fn` gets called with argument 5. As per our `fn` definition, it returns the `innerFn`.

2. This where interesting things happen. When `innerFn` is returned, the JavaScript execution engine sees `innerFn` as a closure and sets its scope accordingly. As we saw in the previous section, closures will have access to the three scope levels. All these three scope levels are set (`arg`, `outer` values will be set in scope level of `innerFn`) when the `innerFn` is returned. The returned function reference is stored in `closureFn`. Thus `closureFn` will have `arg`, `outer` values when called via scope chains.

3. When we finally call the `closureFn`:

   ```
   closureFn()
   ```

   it prints:

   ```
   Visible
   5
   ```

As now you can guess, `closureFn` remembers its context (the scopes; i.e., `outer` and `arg`) when it is born in the second step. Thus the calls to `console.log` print appropriately.

You might be wondering what is the use case of closure?. We have already seen it in action in our `sortBy` function. Let's quickly revisit it.

Revisiting sortBy Function

Recall the sortBy function that we defined and used in the previous chapter:

```
const sortBy = (property) => {
    return (a,b) => {
        var result = (a[property] < b[property]) ? -1 :
        (a[property] > b[property]) ? 1 : 0;
        return result;
    }
}
```

When we called the sortBy function like this:

```
sortBy("firstname")
```

sortBy returned a new function that takes two arguments, like this:

```
(a,b) => { /* implementation */ }
```

Now we are comfortable with closures and we are aware that the returned function will have access to the sortBy function argument property. Because this function will be returned only when sortBy is called, the property argument is linked with a value; hence the returned function will carry this *context* throughout its life:

```
//scope it carries via closure
property = "passedValue"
(a,b) => { /* implementation */ }
```

Now because the returned function carries the value of property in its context, it will use the returned value where it is appropriate and when it is needed. With that explanation in place, we can fully understand closures and higher order functions that allow us to write a function like sortBy that is going to abstract away the inner details. Moving ahead to our functional world.

That's a lot to take in for this section; in the next section we continue our journey of writing more abstract functions using closures and higher order functions.

Higher Order Functions in the Real World (Continued)

With our understanding of closures in place, we can go ahead and implement some useful higher order functions that are used in the real world.

tap Function

Because we are going to deal with lots of functions in the programming world, we need a way to debug what is happening between them. As we have seen in previous chapters, we are designing the functions, which take arguments and return another function, which again takes a few arguments, and so on.

Let's design a simple function called tap:

```
const tap = (value) =>
  (fn) => (
    typeof(fn) === 'function' && fn(value),
    console.log(value)
  )
```

Here the tap function takes a value and returns a function that has the closure over value and it will be executed.

Note   In JavaScript, (exp1,exp2) means it will execute the two arguments and return the result of the second expression, which is exp2. In our preceding example, the syntax will call the function fn and also print the value to the console.

Let's play around with the tap function:

```
tap("fun")((it) => console.log("value is ",it))
=>value is fun
=>fun
```

As you can see in this example, the value **value is fun** gets printed and then the value **fun** is printed. This seems easy and straightforward.

So where can the tap function be used? Imagine you are iterating an array that has data come from a server. You feel that the data are wrong, so you want to debug and see what the array really contains, while iterating. How will you do that? This is where the tap function comes into the picture. For the current scenario, we can do this:

```
forEach([1,2,3], (a) =>
   tap(a)(() =>
     {
       console.log(a)
     }
   )
)
```

This prints the value as expected, providing a simple yet powerful function in our toolkit.

unary Function

There is a default method in the array prototype called map. Don't worry;
we are going to discover numerous functions for arrays in the next chapter,
where we will be seeing how to create our own map, too. For now, map is
a function, which is very similar to the forEach function we have already
defined. The only difference is that map returns the result of the callback
function.

To get the gist of it, let's say we want to double the array and get back
the result; using the map function, we can do that like this:

```
[1, 2, 3].map((a) => { return a * a })
=>[1, 4, 9]
```

The interesting point to note here is that map calls the function with
three arguments, which are element, index, and arr. Imagine we want
to parse the array of strings to the array of int; we have a built-in function
called parseInt that takes two argument parses and radixes and converts
the passed parse into a number if possible. If we pass the parseInt to
our map function, map will pass the index value to the radix argument of
parseInt, which will result in unexpected behavior.

```
['1', '2', '3'].map(parseInt)
=>[1, NaN, NaN]
```

Oops! As you can see in this result, the array [1, NaN, NaN] is not
what we expect. Here we need to convert the parseInt function to another
function that will be expecting only one argument. How can we achieve
that? Meet our next friend, the unary function. The task of the unary
function is to take the given function with n arguments and convert it into
a single argument.

Our unary function looks like the following:

```
const unary = (fn) =>
  fn.length === 1
    ? fn
    : (arg) => fn(arg)
```

We are checking if the passed fn has an argument list of size 1 (which we can find via the length property); if so, we are not going to do anything. If not, we return a new function, which takes only one argument arg and calls the function with that argument.

To see our unary function in action, we can rerun our problem with unary:

```
['1', '2', '3'].map(unary(parseInt))
=>[1, 2, 3]
```

Here our unary function returns a new function (a clone of parseInt), which is going to take only one argument. Thus the map function passing index, arr argument, becomes unaffected as we are getting back the expected result.

Note   There are also functions like binary and others that will convert the function to accept corresponding arguments.

The next two functions that we are going to see are special higher order functions that will allow the developer to control the number of times the function is getting called. They have a lot of use cases in the real world.

once Function

There are a lot of situations in which we need to run a given function only once. This scenario occurs for JavaScript developers in their day-to-day life, as they want to set up a third-party library only once, initiate the payment set up only once, do a bank payment request only once, and so on. These are common cases that developers face.

In this section we are going to write a higher order function called once, which will allow the developer to run the given function only once. Again the point to note here is that we have to keep on abstracting away our day-to-day activities into our functional toolkits.

```
const once = (fn) => {
  let done = false;

  return function () {
    return done ? undefined : ((done = true), fn.apply(this,
    arguments))
  }

}
```

This once function takes an argument fn and returns the result of it by calling it with the apply method (a note on the apply method is given later). The important point to note here is that we have declared a variable called done and set it to false initially. The returned function will have a closure scope over it; hence it will access it to check if done is true, if return undefined else set done to true (thus preventing the next execution), and calling the function with necessary arguments.

Note   The apply function will allow us to set the context for the function and also pass on the arguments for the given function. You can find more about it at https://developer.mozilla.org/en-US/docs/Web/JavaScript/Reference/Global_Objects/Function/apply.

With the once function in place, we can do a quick check of it.

```
var doPayment = once(() => {
    console.log("Payment is done")
})
```

```
doPayment()
=>Payment is done
```

```
//oops bad, we are doing second time!
doPayment()
=>undefined!
```

This code snippet showcases that the doPayment function that is wrapped over once will be executed only once regardless of how many times we call them. The once function is a simple but effective function in our toolkit.

memoize Function

Before we close this section, let's take a look at the function called memoize. We know that the pure function is all about working on its argument and nothing else. It does not depend on the outside world for anything. The results of the pure function are purely based on its argument. Imagine that we have a pure function called factorial, which calculates the factorial for a given number. The function looks like this:

```
var factorial = (n) => {
  if (n === 0) {
    return 1;
  }

  // This is it! Recursion!!
  return n * factorial(n - 1);
}
```

You can quickly check that factorial function with a few inputs:

```
factorial(2)
=>2
factorial(3)
=>6
```

Nothing fancy here. We knew, though, that the factorial of the value 2 is 2, 3 is 6, and so on, mainly because we know the factorial function does work, but only based on its argument and nothing else. This question then arises here: Why can't we store back the result for each input (some sort of an object) and give back the output if the input is already present in the object? Moreover for calculating the factorial for 3, we need to calculate the factorial for 2, so why can't we reuse those calculations in our function? Well, that's exactly what the memoize function is going to do. The memoize function is a special higher order function that allows the function to remember or memorize its result.

Let's see how we can implement such a function in JavaScript. It is as simple as it looks here:

```
const memoized = (fn) => {
  const lookupTable = {};

  return (arg) => lookupTable[arg] || (lookupTable[arg] =
  fn(arg));
}
```

Here we have a local variable called lookupTable that will be in the closure context for the returned function. This will take the argument and check if that argument is in the lookupTable:

```
. . lookupTable[arg] . .
```

If so, return the value; otherwise update the object with new input as a key and the result from fn as its value:

```
(lookupTable[arg] = fn(arg))
```

Perfect. Now we can go and wrap our factorial function into a memoize function to keep remembering its output:

```
let fastFactorial = memoized((n) => {
  if (n === 0) {
    return 1;
  }

  // This is it! Recursion!!
  return n * fastFactorial(n - 1);
})
```

Now go and call fastFactorial:

```
fastFactorial(5)
=>120
=>lookupTable will be like: Object {0: 1, 1: 1, 2: 2, 3: 6,
4: 24, 5: 120}
fastFactorial(3)
=>6 //returned from lookupTable
fastFactorial(7)
=> 5040
=>lookupTable will be like: Object {0: 1, 1: 1, 2: 2, 3: 6,
4: 24, 5: 120, 6: 720, 7: 5040}
```

It is going to work the same way, but now much faster than before. While running fastFactorial, I would like you to inspect the lookupTable object and how it helps in speeding things up as shown in the preceding snippet. That is the beauty of the higher order function: closure and pure functions in action!

Note   Our `memoized` function is written for functions that take only one argument. Can you come up with a solution for all functions with *n* number of arguments?

We have abstracted away many common problems into higher order functions that allowed us to write a solution with elegance and ease.

assign function

JavaScript (JS) objects are mutable, which means the state of the object can be changed after it is created. Often, you will come across a scenario in which you have to merge objects to form a new object. Consider the following objects:

```
var a = {  name: "srikanth" };
var b = {  age: 30 };
var c = {  sex: 'M' };
```

What if I want to merge all objects to create a new object? Let us go ahead and write the relevant function.

```
function objectAssign(target, source) {
    var to = {};
    for (var i = 0; i < arguments.length; i += 1) {
      var from = arguments[i];
      var keys = Object.keys(from);
      for (var j = 0; j < keys.length; j += 1) {
        to[keys[j]] = from[keys[j]];
      }
    }
    return to;
  }
```

`arguments` is a special variable available to every JS function. JS functions allow you to send any number of arguments to a function, which means that if a function is declared with two arguments, JS allows you to send more than two arguments. `Object.keys` is an inbuilt method that gives you the property names of every object, in our case, the name, age, and sex. The following usage shows how we abstracted the functionality to merge any number of JS objects into one object.

```
var customObjectAssign = objectAssign(a, b, c);
//prints { name: 'srikanth', age: 30, sex: 'M' }
```

However, if you're following ES6 standards, you may not have to write a new function. The following function also does the same.

```
// ES6 Object.Assign
var nativeObjectAssign = Object.assign(a, b, c);
//prints { name: 'srikanth', age: 30, sex: 'M' }
```

Note that when we use `Object.assign` to merge objects a, b, and c, even object a is changed. This does not occur with our custom implementation. That is because object a is considered to be the target object we merge into. Because the objects are mutable, a is now updated accordingly. If you require the preceding behavior, you can do this:

```
var nativeObjectAssign = Object.assign({}, a, b, c);
```

Object a will be intact with the preceding usage, because all the objects are merged into an empty object.

Let me show you another new addition to ES6, `Object.entries`. Suppose you have an object such as the following:

```
var book = {
        "id": 111,
        "title": "C# 6.0",
        "author": "ANDREW TROELSEN",
```

```
    "rating": [4.7],
    "reviews": [{good : 4 , excellent : 12}]     };
```

If you're only interested in the title property, the following function can help you convert that property into an array of strings.

```
console.log(Object.entries(book)[1]);
//prints Array ["title", "C# 6.0"]
```

What if you do not want to upgrade to ES6 and yet you're interested in getting object entries? The only way is to implement a functional method that does the same, such as we did earlier. Are you up for the challenge? If yes, I will leave that as an exercise for you.

We have now abstracted away many common problems into higher-order functions that allowed us to write an elegant solution with ease.

Summary

We started this chapter with a set of questions about what a function can see. By starting small and building up examples, we showed how closures make the function remember the context in which it is born. With this understanding in place, we implemented few more higher order functions that are used in the day-to-day life of a JavaScript programmer. Throughout we have seen how to abstract away common problems into a specific function and reuse it. Now we understand the importance of closures, higher order functions, abstraction, and pure functions. In the next chapter we are going to continue building the higher order functions, but with respect to arrays.

CHAPTER 5

Being Functional on Arrays

Welcome to the chapter on arrays and objects. In this chapter we continue our journey of exploring higher order functions that are useful for arrays.

Arrays are used throughout our JavaScript programming world. We use them to store data, manipulate data, find data, and convert (project) the data to another format. In this chapter we are going to see how to improve all these activities using the functional programming techniques we have learned so far.

We create several functions on array, and we solve the common problems functionally rather than imperatively. The functions that we are creating in this chapter might or might not be defined already in the array or object prototype. Be advised that these are for understanding how the real functions themselves work, rather than overriding them.

Note The chapter examples and library source code are in branch chap05. The repo's URL is https://github.com/antoaravinth/functional-es8.git

Once you check out the code, please check out branch chap05:

```
...
git checkout -b chap05 origin/chap05
...
```

© Anto Aravinth, Srikanth Machiraju 2018
A. Aravinth and S. Machiraju, *Beginning Functional JavaScript*,
https://doi.org/10.1007/978-1-4842-4087-8_5

For running the codes, as before run:

...

```
npm run playground
```

...

Working Functionally on Arrays

In this section we create a set of useful functions, and using those functions we solve common problems with Array.

Note   All the functions that we create in this section are called *projecting functions*. Applying a function to an array and creating a new array or new set of value(s) is called a *projection*. The term will make sense when we see our first projecting function map.

---

map

We have already seen how to iterate over the Array using forEach. forEach is a higher order function that is going to iterate over the given array and call the passed function with the current index as its argument. forEach hides away the common problem of iteration, but we cannot use forEach in all cases.

Imagine we want to square all the contents of the array and get back the result in a new array. How can we achieve this using forEach? Using forEach we cannot return the data; instead it just executes the passed function. That's where our first projecting function comes into the picture, and it's called map.

Implementing map is an easy and straightforward task given that we have already seen how to implement forEach itself. The implementation of forEach looks like Listing 5-1.

Listing 5-1. forEach Function Definition

```
const forEach = (array,fn) => {
   for(const value of arr)
      fn(value)
}
```

The map function implementation looks like Listing 5-2.

Listing 5-2. map Function Definition

```
const map = (array,fn) => {
      let results = []
      for(const value of array)
               results.push(fn(value))

      return results;
}
```

The map implementation looks very similar to forEach; it's just that we are capturing the results in a new array as:

. . .

```
      let results = []
```

. . .

and returning the results from the function. Now is a good time to talk about the term *projecting function*. We mentioned earlier that the map function is a projecting function. Why do we call the map function that? The reason is quite simple and straightforward: Because map returns the *transformed* value of the given function, we call it a projecting function. Some people do call map a transforming function, but we are going to stick to the term *projection*.

Now let's solve the problem of squaring the contents of the array using our map function defined in Listing 5-2.

```
map([1,2,3], (x) => x * x)
=>[1,4,9]
```

As you can see in this code snippet, we have achieved our task with simple elegance. Because we are going to create many functions that are specific to the Array type, we are going to wrap all the functions into a const called arrayUtils and then export arrayUtils. It typically looks like Listing 5-3.

Listing 5-3. Wrapping Functions into arrayUtils Object

```
//map function from Listing 5-2
const map = (array,fn) => {
  let results = []
  for(const value of array)
      results.push(fn(value))

  return results;
}

const arrayUtils = {
  map : map
}

export {arrayUtils}

//another file
import arrayUtils from 'lib'
arrayUtils.map //use map

//or

const map = arrayUtils.map
//so that we can call them map
```

Note   In the text we call them map rather than `arrayUtils.map` for clarity purposes.

Perfect. To make the chapter examples more realistic, we are going to build an array of objects, which looks like Listing 5-4.

Listing 5-4. apressBooks Object Describing Book Details

```
let apressBooks = [
        {
                "id": 111,
                "title": "C# 6.0",
                "author": "ANDREW TROELSEN",
                "rating": [4.7],
                "reviews": [{good : 4 , excellent : 12}]
        },
        {
                "id": 222,
                "title": "Efficient Learning Machines",
                "author": "Rahul Khanna",
                "rating": [4.5],
                "reviews": []
        },
        {
                "id": 333,
                "title": "Pro AngularJS",
                "author": "Adam Freeman",
                "rating": [4.0],
                "reviews": []
        },
```

```
        {
                "id": 444,
                "title": "Pro ASP.NET",
                "author": "Adam Freeman",
                "rating": [4.2],
                "reviews": [{good : 14 , excellent : 12}]
        }
];
```

Note   This array does contain real titles that are published by
Apress, but the review key values are my own interpretations.

All the functions that we are going to create in this chapter will be run
for the given array of objects. Now suppose we need to get the array of an
object that only has a title and author name in it. How are we going to
achieve the same thing using the map function? Do you see a solution in
your mind?

The solution is simple using the map function, which looks like this:

```
map(apressBooks,(book) => {
        return {title: book.title,author:book.author}
})
```

That code is going to return the result as you would expect. The object
in the returned array will have only two properties: One is title and the
other one is author, as you specified in your function:

```
[ { title: 'C# 6.0', author: 'ANDREW TROELSEN' },
  { title: 'Efficient Learning Machines', author: 'Rahul Khanna' },
  { title: 'Pro AngularJS', author: 'Adam Freeman' },
  { title: 'Pro ASP.NET', author: 'Adam Freeman' } ]
```

We do not always just want to transform all our array contents into a new one. Rather, we want to filter the content of the array and then perform the transformation. It is time now to meet the next function in the queue, filter.

filter

Imagine we want to get the list of books with ratings higher than 4.5. How we are going to achieve this? It is definitely not a problem for map to solve, but we need a function similar to map that just checks a condition, before pushing the results into the results array.

Let's first take another look at the map function (from Listing 5-2):

```
const map = (array,fn) => {
  let results = []
  for(const value of array)
      results.push(fn(value))

  return results;
}
```

Here we need to check a condition or predicate before we do this:

```
. . .
        results.push(fn(value))
. . .
```

Let's add that into a separate function called filter as shown in Listing 5-5.

Listing 5-5. filter Function Definition

```
const filter = (array,fn) => {
  let results = []
  for(const value of array)
    (fn(value)) ? results.push(value) : undefined

  return results;
}
```

With the `filter` function in place, we can solve our problem at hand in the following way:

```
filter(apressBooks, (book) => book.rating[0] > 4.5)
```

which is going to return the expected result:

```
[ { id: 111,
    title: 'C# 6.0',
    author: 'ANDREW TROELSEN',
    rating: [ 4.7 ],
    reviews: [ [Object] ] } ]
```

We are constantly improving the method to deal with arrays using these higher order functions. Before we go further with the next functions on the array, we are going to see how to chain the projection functions (`map`, `filter`) to get the desired results in complex situations.

Chaining Operations

It's always the case that we need to *chain* several functions to achieve our goal. For example, imagine the problem of getting the `title` and `author` objects out of our `apressBooks` array for which the review value is greater than `4.5`. The initial step to tackle this problem is to solve it via `map` and `filter`. In that case, the code might look like this:

```
let goodRatingBooks =
 filter(apressBooks, (book) => book.rating[0] > 4.5)

map(goodRatingBooks,(book) => {
        return {title: book.title,author:book.author}
})
```

which is going to return the result as expected:

```
[ {
        title: 'C# 6.0',
    author: 'ANDREW TROELSEN'
        }
]
```

An important point to note here is that both map and filter are projection functions, so they always return data after applying the transformation (via the passed higher order function) on the array. We can therefore chain both filter and map (the order is very important) to get the task done without the need for additional variables (i.e., goodRatingBooks):

```
map(filter(apressBooks, (book) => book.rating[0] > 4.5),(book)
=> {
        return {title: book.title,author:book.author}
})
```

This code literally tells the problem we are solving: "Map over the filtered array whose rating is 4.5 and return their title and author keys in an object." Due to the nature of both map and filter, we have abstracted away the details of the array themselves, and we started focusing on the problem at hand.

We show examples of chaining methods in the upcoming sections.

Note   We will see another way to achieve the same thing via function composition later.

---

concatAll

Let's now tweak the apressBooks array a bit, so that we have a data structure that looks like the one shown in Listing 5-6.

Listing 5-6.   Updated apressBooks Object with Book Details

```
let apressBooks = [
        {
                name : "beginners",
                bookDetails : [
                        {
                                "id": 111,
                                "title": "C# 6.0",
                                "author": "ANDREW TROELSEN",
                                "rating": [4.7],
                                "reviews": [{good : 4 ,
                                excellent : 12}]
                        },
                        {

                                "id": 222,
                                "title": "Efficient Learning
                                Machines",
                                "author": "Rahul Khanna",
                                "rating": [4.5],
                                "reviews": []
                        }
                ]
        },
```

```
{
    name : "pro",
    bookDetails : [
                    {
                        "id": 333,
                        "title": "Pro AngularJS",
                        "author": "Adam Freeman",
                        "rating": [4.0],
                        "reviews": []
                    },
                    {
                        "id": 444,
                        "title": "Pro ASP.NET",
                        "author": "Adam Freeman",
                        "rating": [4.2],
                        "reviews": [{good : 14 ,
                        excellent : 12}]
                    }
                 ]
    }
];
```

Now let's take up the same problem that we saw in the previous section: getting the title and author for the books with ratings above 4.5. We can start solving the problem by first mapping over data:

```
map(apressBooks,(book) => {
        return book.bookDetails
})
```

That is going to return us this value:

```
[ [ { id: 111,
      title: 'C# 6.0',
      author: 'ANDREW TROELSEN',
      rating: [Object],
      reviews: [Object] },
    { id: 222,
      title: 'Efficient Learning Machines',
      author: 'Rahul Khanna',
      rating: [Object],
      reviews: [] } ],
  [ { id: 333,
      title: 'Pro AngularJS',
      author: 'Adam Freeman',
      rating: [Object],
      reviews: [] },
    { id: 444,
      title: 'Pro ASP.NET',
      author: 'Adam Freeman',
      rating: [Object],
      reviews: [Object] } ] ]
```

As you can see, the return data from our map function contains Array inside Array because our bookDetails itself is an array. Now if we pass these data to our filter, we are going to have problems, as filters cannot work on nested arrays.

That's where the concatAll function comes in. The job of concatAll is simple enough: It needs to concatenate all the nested arrays into a single array. You can also call concatAll as a flatten method. The implementation of concatAll looks like Listing 5-7.

Listing 5-7. concatAll Function Definition

```
const concatAll = (array,fn) => {
  let results = []
  for(const value of array)
    results.push.apply(results, value);

  return results;
}
```

Here we just pushed up the inner array while iterating into our results array.

Note We have used JavaScript Function's `apply` method to set the push context to `results` itself and pass the argument as the current index of the iteration - `value`.

The main goal of `concatAll` is to unnest the nested arrays into a single array. The following code explains the concept in action:

```
concatAll(
        map(apressBooks,(book) => {
                return book.bookDetails
        })
)
```

That is going to return us the result we expected:

```
[ { id: 111,
    title: 'C# 6.0',
    author: 'ANDREW TROELSEN',
    rating: [ 4.7 ],
    reviews: [ [Object] ] },
```

```
{ id: 222,
  title: 'Efficient Learning Machines',
  author: 'Rahul Khanna',
  rating: [ 4.5 ],
  reviews: [] },
{ id: 333,
  title: 'Pro AngularJS',
  author: 'Adam Freeman',
  rating: [ 4 ],
  reviews: [] },
{ id: 444,
  title: 'Pro ASP.NET',
  author: 'Adam Freeman',
  rating: [ 4.2 ],
  reviews: [ [Object] ] } ]
```

Now we can go ahead and easily do a `filter` with our condition like this:

```
let goodRatingCriteria = (book) => book.rating[0] > 4.5;
filter(
        concatAll(
                map(apressBooks,(book) => {
                        return book.bookDetails
                })
        )
,goodRatingCriteria)
```

That is going to return the expected value:

```
[ { id: 111,
    title: 'C# 6.0',
    author: 'ANDREW TROELSEN',
    rating: [ 4.7 ],
    reviews: [ [Object] ] } ]
```

We have seen how designing a higher order function within the world of the array does solve a lot of problems in elegant fashion. We have done a really good job up to now. We still have to see a few more functions with respect to arrays in the upcoming sections.

Reducing Function

If you talk about functional programming anywhere, you often hear the term *reduce functions*. What are they? Why they are so useful? reduce is a beautiful function that is designed to showcase the power of closure in JavaScript. In this section, we are going to explore the usefulness of reducing an array.

reduce Function

To give a solid example of the reduce function and where it's been used, let's look at the problem of finding the summation of the given array. To start, suppose we have an array called":

```
let useless = [2,5,6,1,10]
```

We need to find the sum of the given array, but how we can achieve that? A simple solution would be the following:

```
let result = 0;
forEach(useless,(value) => {
   result = result + value;
})
console.log(result)
=> 24
```

With this problem, we are reducing the array (which has several data) into a single value. We start with a simple *accumulator*; in this case we call it as result to store our summation result while traversing the array itself. Note that we have set the result value to default 0 in case of summation. What if we need to find the product of all the elements in the given array? In that case we will be setting the result value to 1. This whole process of setting up the accumulator and traversing the array (remembering the previous value of accumulator) to produce a single element is called reducing an array.

Because we are going to repeat this process for all array-reducing operations, can't we abstract these into a function? You can, and that's where the reduce function comes in. The implementation of the reduce function looks like Listing 5-8.

Listing 5-8. reduce Function First Implementation

```
const reduce = (array,fn) => {
        let accumlator = 0;
        for(const value of array)
                accumlator = fn(accumlator,value)

        return [accumlator]
}
```

Now with the reduce function in place, we can solve our summation problem using it like this:

```
reduce(useless,(acc,val) => acc + val)
=>[24]
```

That is great, but what if we want to find a product of the given array? The reduce function is going to fail, mainly because we are using an accumulator value to 0. So, our product result will be 0, too:

```
reduce(useless,(acc,val) => acc * val)
=>[0]
```

We can solve this by rewriting the reduce function from Listing 5-8 such that it takes an argument for setting up the initial value for the accumulator. Let's do this right away in Listing 5-9.

Listing 5-9. reduce Function Final Implementation

```
const reduce = (array,fn,initialValue) => {
        let accumlator;

        if(initialValue != undefined)
                accumlator = initialValue;
        else
                accumlator = array[0];

        if(initialValue === undefined)
                for(let i=1;i<array.length;i++)
                        accumlator = fn(accumlator,array[i])
        else
                for(const value of array)
                accumlator = fn(accumlator,value)
        return [accumlator]
}
```

We have made the changes to the reduce function so that now if initialValue is not passed, the reduce function will take the first element in the array as its accumulator value.

Note   Have a look at the two for loop statements. When initialValue is undefined, we need to start looping the array from the second element, as the first value of the accumulator will be used as the initial value. If initialValue is passed by the caller, then we need to iterate the full array.

Now let's try our product problem using the reduce function:

```
reduce(useless,(acc,val) => acc * val,1)
=>[600]
```

Next we'll use reduce in our running example, apressBooks.
Bringing apressBooks (updated in Listing 5-6) in here, for easy reference,
we have this:

```
let apressBooks = [
        {
                name : "beginners",
                bookDetails : [
                        {
                                "id": 111,
                                "title": "C# 6.0",
                                "author": "ANDREW TROELSEN",
                                "rating": [4.7],
                                "reviews": [{good : 4 ,
                                excellent : 12}]
                        },
                        {

                                "id": 222,
                                "title": "Efficient Learning
                                Machines",
                                "author": "Rahul Khanna",
                                "rating": [4.5],
                                "reviews": []
                        }
                ]
        },
```

```
    {
        name : "pro",
        bookDetails : [
                    {
                            "id": 333,
                            "title": "Pro AngularJS",
                            "author": "Adam Freeman",
                            "rating": [4.0],
                            "reviews": []
                    },
                    {
                            "id": 444,
                            "title": "Pro ASP.NET",
                            "author": "Adam Freeman",
                            "rating": [4.2],
                            "reviews": [{good : 14 ,
                            excellent : 12}]
                    }
            ]
        }
];
```

On a good day, your boss comes to your desk and asks you to implement the logic of finding the number of good and excellent reviews from our apressBooks. You think this is a perfect problem that can be solved easily via the reduce function. Remember that apressBooks contains an array inside an array (as we saw in the previous section), so we need to concatAll to make it a flat array. Because reviews are a part of bookDetails, we don't name a key, so we can just map bookDetails and concatAll in the following way:

```
concatAll(
        map(apressBooks,(book) => {
                return book.bookDetails
        })
)
```

Now let's solve our problem using reduce:

```
let bookDetails = concatAll(
        map(apressBooks,(book) => {
                return book.bookDetails
        })
)
reduce(bookDetails,(acc,bookDetail) => {
        let goodReviews = bookDetail.reviews[0] != undefined ?
        bookDetail.reviews[0].good : 0
        let excellentReviews = bookDetail.reviews[0] !=
        undefined ? bookDetail.reviews[0].excellent : 0
        return {good: acc.good + goodReviews,excellent :
        acc.excellent + excellentReviews}
},{good:0,excellent:0})
```

That is going to return the following result:

```
[ { good: 18, excellent: 24 } ]
```

Now let's walk through the reduce function to see how this magic happened. The first point to note here is that we are passing an accumulator to an initialValue, which is nothing but:

```
{good:0,excellent:0}
```

In the reduce function body, we are getting the good and excellent review details (from our bookDetail object) and storing them in the corresponding variables, namely goodReviews and excellentReviews:

```
let goodReviews = bookDetail.reviews[0] != undefined ?
bookDetail.reviews[0].good : 0
let excellentReviews = bookDetail.reviews[0] != undefined ?
bookDetail.reviews[0].excellent : 0
```

With that in place, we can walk through the reduce function call trace to understand better what's happening. For the first iteration, goodReviews and excellentReviews will be the following:

```
goodReviews = 4
excellentReviews = 12
```

and our accumulator will be the following:

```
{good:0,excellent:0}
```

as we have passed the initial line. Once the reduce function executes the line:

```
  return {good: acc.good + goodReviews,excellent : acc.
excellent + excellentReviews}
```

our internal accumulator value gets changed to:

```
{good:4,excellent:12}
```

We are now done with the first iteration of our array. In the second and third iterations, we don't have reviews; hence, both goodReviews and excellentReviews will be 0, but not affecting our accumulator value, which remains the same:

```
{good:4,excellent:12}
```

In our fourth and final iteration, we will be having goodReviews and excellentReviews as:

```
goodReviews = 14
excellentReviews = 12
```

and the accumulator value being:

```
{good:4,excellent:12}
```

Now when we execute the line:

```
return {good: acc.good + goodReviews,excellent : acc.excellent + excellentReviews}
```

our accumulator value changes to:

```
{good:18,excellent:28}
```

Because we are done iterating all our array content, the latest accumulator value will be returned, which is the result.

As you can see here, in this process we have abstracted away internal details into higher order functions, leading to elegant code. Before we close this chapter, let's implement the zip function, which is another useful function.

Zipping Arrays

Life is not always as easy as you think. We had reviews within our bookDetails in our apressBooks details such that we could easily work with it. However, if data like apressBooks does come from the server, they do return data like reviews as a separate array, rather than the embedded data, which will look like Listing 5-10.

Listing 5-10. Splitting the apressBooks Object

```
let apressBooks = [
        {
                name : "beginners",
                bookDetails : [
                        {
                                "id": 111,
                                "title": "C# 6.0",
                                "author": "ANDREW TROELSEN",
                                "rating": [4.7]
                        },
                        {

                                "id": 222,
                                "title": "Efficient Learning
                                Machines",
                                "author": "Rahul Khanna",
                                "rating": [4.5],
                                "reviews": []

                        }
                ]
        },
        {
            name : "pro",
            bookDetails : [
                        {
                                "id": 333,
                                "title": "Pro AngularJS",
                                "author": "Adam Freeman",
                                "rating": [4.0],
                                "reviews": []
                        },
```

```
                        {
                                "id": 444,
                                "title": "Pro ASP.NET",
                                "author": "Adam Freeman",
                                "rating": [4.2]
                        }
                ]
        }
];
```

Listing 5-11. reviewDetails Object Contains Review Details of the Book

```
let reviewDetails = [
        {
                "id": 111,
                "reviews": [{good : 4 , excellent : 12}]
        },
        {
                "id" : 222,
                "reviews" : []
        },
        {
                "id" : 333,
                "reviews" : []
        },
        {
                "id" : 444,
                "reviews": [{good : 14 , excellent : 12}]
        }
]
```

In Listing 5-11, the reviews are fleshed out into a separate array; they are matched with the book id. It's a typical example of how data are segregated into different parts. How do we work with these sorts of split data?

zip Function

The task of the zip function is to merge two given arrays. In our example, we need to merge both apressBooks and reviewDetails into a single array, so that we have all necessary data under a single tree.

The implementation of zip looks like Listing 5-12.

Listing 5-12. zip Function Definition

```
const zip = (leftArr,rightArr,fn) => {
        let index, results = [];

        for(index = 0;index < Math.min(leftArr.length,
        rightArr.length);index++)
                results.push(fn(leftArr[index],rightArr[index]));

        return results;
}
```

zip is a very simple function; we just iterate over the two given arrays. Because here we are dealing with two array details, we get the minimum length of the given two arrays using Math.min:

. . .

```
Math.min(leftArr.length, rightArr.length)
```

. . .

Once you get the minimum length, we call our passed higher order function fn with the current leftArr value and rightArr value.

Suppose we want to add the two contents of the array; we can do so via zip like the following:

```
zip([1,2,3],[4,5,6],(x,y) => x+y)
=> [5,7,9]
```

Now let's solve the same problem that we have solved in the previous section: Find the total count of good and excellent reviews for the Apress collection. Because the data are split into two different structures, we are going to use zip to solve our current problem:

```
//same as before get the
//bookDetails
let bookDetails = concatAll(
        map(apressBooks,(book) => {
                return book.bookDetails
        })
)

//zip the results
let mergedBookDetails = zip(bookDetails,reviewDetails,
(book,review) => {
  if(book.id === review.id)
  {
    let clone = Object.assign({},book)
    clone.ratings = review
    return clone
  }
})
```

Let's break down what's happening in the zip function. The result of the zip function is nothing but the same old data structure we had, precisely, mergedBookDetails:

```
[ { id: 111,
    title: 'C# 6.0',
    author: 'ANDREW TROELSEN',
    rating: [ 4.7 ],
    ratings: { id: 111, reviews: [Object] } },
  { id: 222,
    title: 'Efficient Learning Machines',
    author: 'Rahul Khanna',
    rating: [ 4.5 ],
    reviews: [],
    ratings: { id: 222, reviews: [] } },
  { id: 333,
    title: 'Pro AngularJS',
    author: 'Adam Freeman',
    rating: [ 4 ],
    reviews: [],
    ratings: { id: 333, reviews: [] } },
  { id: 444,
    title: 'Pro ASP.NET',
    author: 'Adam Freeman',
    rating: [ 4.2 ],
    ratings: { id: 444, reviews: [Object] } } ]
```

The way we have arrived at this result is very simple; while doing the zip operation we are taking the bookDetails array and reviewDetails array. We are checking if both the ids match, and if so we clone a new object out of the book and call it clone:

. . .

```
let clone = Object.assign({},book)
```

. . .

Now `clone` gets a copy of what's there in the book object. Howe,ver, the important point to note is that `clone` is pointing to a separate reference. Adding or manipulating `clone` doesn't change the real book reference itself. In JavaScript, objects are used by reference, so changing the book object by default within our `zip` function will affect the contents of `bookDetails` itself, which we don't want to do.

Once we took up the `clone`, we added to it a `ratings` key with the `review` object as its value:

```
clone.ratings = review
```

Finally, we are returning it. Now you can apply the `reduce` function as before to solve the problem. `zip` is yet another small and simple function, but its uses are very powerful.

Summary

We have made a lot of progress in this chapter. We created several useful functions such as `map`, `filter`, `concatAll`, `reduce`, and `zip` to make it easier to work with arrays. We term these functions projection functions, as these functions always return the array after applying the transformation (which is passed via a higher order function). An important point to keep in mind is that these are just higher order functions, which we will be using in daily tasks. Understanding how these functions work helps us to think in more functional terms, but our functional journey is not yet over.

Having created many useful functions on arrays in this chapter, in the next one we will be discussing the concepts of currying and partial application. These terms are nothing to fear; they are simple concepts but become very powerful when put into action. See you in Chapter 6.

CHAPTER 6

Currying and Partial Application

In this chapter we are going to see what the term *currying* means. Once we understand what this means and where it can be used, we will move onto another concept in functional programming called *partial application.* Both currying and partial application are important to understand as we use them during functional composition. As in the previous chapters, we are going to look at a sample problem and explain how functional programming techniques like currying and partial application can be applied.

Note   The chapter examples and library source code are in branch chap06. The repo's URL is https://github.com/antoaravinth/functional-es8.git.

Once you check out the code, please check out branch chap06:

```
...
git checkout -b chap06 origin/chap06
...
```

For running the codes, as before run:

```
...
npm run playground
...
```

© Anto Aravinth, Srikanth Machiraju 2018
A. Aravinth and S. Machiraju, *Beginning Functional JavaScript*,
https://doi.org/10.1007/978-1-4842-4087-8_6

A Few Notes on Terminology

Before explaining what currying and partial application mean, we need to understand a few terms that we will be using in this chapter.

Unary Function

A function is called *unary* if it takes a single function argument. For example, the identity function, shown in Listing 6-1, is a unary function.

Listing 6-1. Unary identity Function

```
const identity = (x) => x;
```

This function takes only one argument, x, so we can call it a unary function.

Binary Function

A function is called *binary* if it takes two arguments. For example, in Listing 6-2, the add function is a binary function.

Listing 6-2. Binary add Function

```
const add = (x,y) => x + y;
```

The add function takes two arguments, x,y; hence we call it a binary function.

As you can guess, there are ternary functions that take three arguments, and so on. JavaScript also allows a special type of function that we call a *variadic* function, which takes a variable number of arguments.

Variadic Functions

A variadic function is a function that takes a variable number of arguments. Remember that we had arguments in older versions of JavaScript, which we can use to capture the variable number of arguments.

Listing 6-3. Variadic Function

```
function variadic(a){
        console.log(a);
        console.log(arguments)
}
```

We call the variadic function like this:

```
variadic(1,2,3)
=> 1
=> [1,2,3]
```

Note   As you can see in the output, arguments do capture all the arguments that are passed to a function.

As you can see in Listing 6-3, using arguments we are able to capture the additional arguments one could call on a function. Using this technique, we used to achieve the variadic functions in ES5 versions. However, starting with ES6, we have an operator called *Spread Operator* that we can use to achieve the same result.

Listing 6-4. Variadic Function Using Spread Operator

```
const variadic = (a,...variadic) => {
        console.log(a)
        console.log(variadic)
}
```

Now if we call this function we get exactly what we would expect:

```
variadic(1,2,3)
=> 1
=> [2,3]
```

As you can see in the result, we were pointed to the first passed argument 1 and all other remaining arguments captured by our `variadic` variable that uses the **. . .** rest argument! ES6 style is more concise as it clearly mentions that a function does take variadic arguments for processing.

Now that we have some common terms in mind with respect to functions, it's time to turn our attention to the fancy term currying.

Currying

Have you heard the term *currying n* number of times from the blogs and still wonder what it means? Don't worry; we are going to break the currying definition into smaller definitions, which will make sense to you.

We'll start with a simple question: What is currying? A simple answer to that question would be this: Currying is a process of converting a function with *n* number of arguments into a *nested* unary function. Don't worry if that doesn't make sense to you yet. Let's see what it means using a simple example.

Imagine we have a function called add:

```
const add = (x,y) => x + y;
```

It's a simple function. We can call this function like `add(1,1)`, which is going to give the result 2. Nothing fancy there. Now here is the curried version of the add function:

```
const addCurried = x => y => x + y;
```

The `addCurried` function is now a curried version of add. If we call `addCurried` with a single argument like this:

```
addCurried(4)
```

it returns a function where x value is captured via the closure concept as we saw in earlier chapters:

```
=> fn = y => 4 + y
```

We can call the addCurried function like this to get the proper result:

```
addCurried(4)(4)
=> 8
```

Here we have manually converted the add function, which takes the two arguments into an addCurried function, which has nested unary functions. The process of converting a function from two arguments to a function that takes one argument (unary function) is called currying, as shown in Listing 6-5.

Listing 6-5. curry Function Definition

```
const curry = (binaryFn) => {
  return function (firstArg) {
    return function (secondArg) {
      return binaryFn(firstArg, secondArg);
    };
  };
};
```

Note   We have written the curry function in ES5 format so that we can visualize the process of returning a *nested* unary function.

Now we can use our curry function to convert the add function to a curried version like this:

```
let autoCurriedAdd = curry(add)
autoCurriedAdd(2)(2)
=> 4
```

The output is exactly what we wanted to get. Now it's time to revise the definition of currying: Currying is a process of converting a function with n number of arguments into a nested unary function.

As you can see in our curry function definition, we are converting the binary function into nested functions, each of which takes only one argument; that is, we are returning the nested unary functions. Now we have clarified the term currying in your head, but the obvious questions you still have are these: Why do we need currying? What is its use?

Currying Use Cases

We'll start simple. Imagine we have to create a function for creating tables. For example, we need to create tableOf2, tableOf3, tableOf4, and so on. We can achieve this via Listing 6-6.

Listing 6-6. tables Function Without Currying

```
const tableOf2 = (y) => 2 * y
const tableOf3 = (y) => 3 * y
const tableOf4 = (y) => 4 * y
```

With that in place, the functions can be called this:

```
tableOf2(4)
=> 8
tableOf3(4)
=> 12
tableOf4(4)
=> 16
```

Now you see that you can generalize the tables concept into a single function like this:

```
const genericTable = (x,y) => x * y
```

and then you can use genericTable to get tableOf2 like the following:

```
genericTable(2,2)
genericTable(2,3)
genericTable(2,4)
```

and the same for tableOf3 and tableOf4. If you notice the pattern, we are filling up 2 in the first argument for tableOf2, 3 for tableOf3, and so on! Perhaps you are thinking that we can solve this problem via curry? Let's build tables from genericTable using curry:

Listing 6-7. tables Function Using Currying

```
const tableOf2 = curry(genericTable)(2)
const tableOf3 = curry(genericTable)(3)
const tableOf4 = curry(genericTable)(4)
```

Now you can do your testing with these curried versions of the tables:

```
console.log("Tables via currying")
console.log("2 * 2 =",tableOf2(2))
console.log("2 * 3 =",tableOf2(3))
console.log("2 * 4 =",tableOf2(4))

console.log("3 * 2 =",tableOf3(2))
console.log("3 * 3 =",tableOf3(3))
console.log("3 * 4 =",tableOf3(4))

console.log("4 * 2 =",tableOf4(2))
console.log("4 * 3 =",tableOf4(3))
console.log("4 * 4 =",tableOf4(4))
```

This is going to print the value we expect:

```
Table via currying
2 * 2 = 4
2 * 3 = 6
2 * 4 = 8
3 * 2 = 6
3 * 3 = 9
3 * 4 = 12
4 * 2 = 8
4 * 3 = 12
4 * 4 = 16
```

A logger Function: Using Currying

The example in the previous section helped us understand what currying does, but let's use a more complicated example in this section. As developers when we write code, we do a lot of logging at several stages of the application. We could write a helper logger function that looks like Listing 6-8.

Listing 6-8. Simple loggerHelper Function

```
const loggerHelper = (mode,initialMessage,errorMessage,lineNo)
=> {
        if(mode === "DEBUG")
                console.debug(initialMessage,errorMessage +
                "at line: " + lineNo)
        else if(mode === "ERROR")
                console.error(initialMessage,errorMessage +
                "at line: " + lineNo)
```

```
else if(mode === "WARN")
        console.warn(initialMessage,errorMessage +
        "at line: " + lineNo)
else
        throw "Wrong mode"
}
```

When any developer needs to print an error to the console from the Stats.js file, he or she can use the function like the following:

```
loggerHelper("ERROR","Error At Stats.js","Invalid argument
passed",23)
loggerHelper("ERROR","Error At Stats.js","undefined argument",223)
loggerHelper("ERROR","Error At Stats.js","curry function is not
defined",3)
loggerHelper("ERROR","Error At Stats.js","slice is not
defined",31)
```

Similarly, we can use the loggerHelper function for debug and warn messages. As you can tell, we are repeating the arguments, mainly mode and initialMessage, for all the calls. Can we do it better? Yes, we can do these calls better via currying. Can we use our curry function that is defined in the previous section? Unfortunately, no, because the curry function that we have designed can handle only binary functions, not a function like loggerHelper that takes four arguments.

Let us solve this problem and implement the fully functional curry function, which handles any function with n number of arguments.

Revisit Curry

We all know that we can curry (Listing 6-5) only a function. How about many functions? It's simple but important to have it in our implementation of curry. Let's add the rule first, as shown in Listing 6-9.

Listing 6-9. Revisting curry Function Definition

```
let curry =(fn) => {
    if(typeof fn!=='function'){
        throw Error('No function provided');
    }
};
```

With that check in place, if others call our curry function with an integer like 2, and so on, they get back the error. That's perfect! The next requirement to our curried function is that if anyone provided all arguments to a curried function, we need to execute the real function by passing the arguments. Let's add that using Listing 6-10.

Listing 6-10. curry Function Handling Arguments

```
let curry =(fn) => {
    if(typeof fn!=='function'){
        throw Error('No function provided');
    }

    return function curriedFn(...args){
      return fn.apply(null, args);
    };
};
```

Now if we have a function called multiply:

```
const multiply = (x,y,z) => x * y * z;
```

We can use our new curry function like the following:

```
curry(multiply)(1,2,3)
=> 6
curry(multiply)(1,2,0)
=> 0
```

118

Let's look at how it really works. We have added the logic in our curry function like this:

```
return function curriedFn(...args){
        return fn.apply(null, args);
};
```

The returned function is a variadic function, which returns the function result by calling the function via apply along by passing the args:

```
. . .
fn.apply(null, args);
. . .
```

With our curry(multiply)(1,2,3) example, args will be pointing to [1,2,3] and because we are calling apply on fn, it's equivalent to:

```
multiply(1,2,3)
```

which is exactly what we wanted! Thus, we get back the expected result from the function.

Now let us get back to the problem of converting the *n* argument function into a nested unary function (that's the definition of curry itself)!

Listing 6-11. curry Function Converting n arg Function to Unary Function

```
let curry =(fn) => {
    if(typeof fn!=='function'){
        throw Error('No function provided');
    }

    return function curriedFn(...args){
```

```
    if(args.length < fn.length){
      return function(){
        return curriedFn.apply(null, args.concat( [].slice.
        call(arguments) ));
      };
    }
    return fn.apply(null, args);
  };
};
```

We have added the part:

```
if(args.length < fn.length){
        return function(){
            return curriedFn.apply(null, args.concat( [].slice.
            call(arguments) ));
        };
}
```

Let's understand what's happening in this piece of code, one element at a time.

```
args.length < fn.length
```

This line checks if the argument that is passed via . . . args length and the function argument list length is less or not. If so we go into the if block, or else we fall back to call the full function as before.

Once we enter the if block, we use the apply function to call curriedFn recursively like this:

```
curriedFn.apply(null, args.concat( [].slice.call(arguments) ));
```

The snippet

```
args.concat( [].slice.call(arguments) )
```

is important. Using the concat function, we are concatenating the arguments that are passed one at a time and calling the curriedFn recursively. Because we are combining all the passed arguments and calling it recursively, we will meet a point in which the line

```
if (args.length < fn.length)
```

condition fails. The argument list length (args) and function argument length (fn.length) will be equal, thus skipping the if block and calling

```
return fn.apply(null, args);
```

which is going to yield the function's full result!

With that understanding in place, we can use our curry function to invoke the multiply function:

```
curry(multiply)(3)(2)(1)
=> 6
```

Perfect! We have created our own curry function.

Note   You can call the preceding code snippet like the following, too:

```
let curriedMul3 = curry(multiply)(3)
let curriedMul2 = curriedMul3(2)
let curriedMul1 = curriedMul2(1)
```

where curriedMul1 will be equal to 6. We use curry(multiply)(3)(2)(1), though, as it is much more readable.

An important point to note is that our curry function is now converting a function of *n* arguments into a function that can be called as a unary function as the example shows.

Back to logger Function

Now let's solve our logger function using the defined curry function. Bringing up the function here for easy reference (Listing 6-8):

```
const loggerHelper = (mode,initialMessage,errorMessage,lineNo) => {
        if(mode === "DEBUG")
                console.debug(initialMessage,errorMessage +
                "at line: " + lineNo)
        else if(mode === "ERROR")
                console.error(initialMessage,errorMessage +
                "at line: " + lineNo)
        else if(mode === "WARN")
                console.warn(initialMessage,errorMessage +
                "at line: " + lineNo)
        else
                throw "Wrong mode"
}
```

The developer used to call the function:

```
loggerHelper("ERROR","Error At Stats.js","Invalid argument
passed",23)
```

Now let's solve the repeating first two arguments problem via curry:

```
let errorLogger = curry(loggerHelper)("ERROR")("Error At
Stats.js");
let debugLogger = curry(loggerHelper)("DEBUG")("Debug At
Stats.js");
let warnLogger = curry(loggerHelper)("WARN")("Warn At
Stats.js");
```

Now we can easily refer to the earlier curried functions and use them under the respective context:

```
//for error
errorLogger("Error message",21)
=> Error At Stats.js Error messageat line: 21
```

```
//for debug
debugLogger("Debug message",233)
=> Debug At Stats.js Debug messageat line: 233
```

```
//for warn
warnLogger("Warn message",34)
=> Warn At Stats.js Warn messageat line: 34
```

That's brilliant! We have seen how the curry function helps in the real world to remove a lot of boilerplates in function calls. Don't forget to thank the closures concept, which is backing up the curry function. The debug module of the node uses the curry concept in its API (see https://github.com/visionmedia/debug).

Currying in Action

In the previous section we created our own curry function. We have also seen a simple example of using this curry function.

In this section we are going to see small but compact examples in which the currying technique is used. The examples shown in this section will help you better understand how to use currying in your day-to-day activities.

Finding a Number in Array Contents

Imagine we want to find the array content that has a number. We can solve the problem via the following code snippet:

```
let match = curry(function(expr, str) {
  return str.match(expr);
});
```

The returned match function is a curried function. We can give the first argument expr a regular expression /[0-9]+/ that will indicate whether the content has a number in it.

```
let hasNumber = match(/[0-9]+/)
```

Now we will create a curried filter function:

```
let filter = curry(function(f, ary) {
  return ary.filter(f);
});
```

With hasNumber and filter in place, we can create a new function called findNumbersInArray:

```
let findNumbersInArray = filter(hasNumber)
```

Now you can test it:

```
findNumbersInArray(["js","number1"])
=> ["number1"]
```

Squaring an Array

We know how to square contents of an array. We have also seen the same problem in previous chapters. We use the map function and pass on the square function to achieve the solution to our problem. Here we can use the curry function to solve the same problem in another way:

```
let map = curry(function(f, ary) {
  return ary.map(f);
});

let squareAll = map((x) => x * x)

squareAll([1,2,3])
=> [1,4,9]
```

As you can see in this example, we have created a new function, squareAll, that we can now use elsewhere in our code base. Similarly you can also do this for findEvenOfArray, findPrimeOfArray, and so on.

Data Flow

In both sections on using currying, we have designed the curried functions such that they always take the array at the end. This is an intentional way of creating a curried function. As discussed in previous chapters, we as programmers often work on data structures like array, so making the array as the last argument allows us to create lot of reusable functions like squareAll and findNumbersInArray that we can use throughout the code base.

Note   In our source code companion, we have called the curry function curryN. It's just to keep the old curry as is, which was supposed to do currying on binary functions.

Partial Application

In this section we are going to see yet another function called partial that allows developers to apply the function arguments partially.

Imagine we want to perform a set of operations every 10 milliseconds. Using the setTimeout function, we can do this:

```
setTimeout(() => console.log("Do X task"),10);
setTimeout(() => console.log("Do Y task"),10);
```

As you can see, we are passing on 10 for every one of our setTimeout function calls. Can we hide that from the code? Can we use a curry function to solve this problem? The answer is no, because the curry function applies the argument from the leftmost to rightmost lists. Because we want to pass on the functions as needed and keep 10 as a constant (which is most of the argument list), we cannot use curry as such. One workaround is that we can wrap our setTimeout function so that the function argument becomes the rightmost one:

```
const setTimeoutWrapper = (time,fn) => {
  setTimeout(fn,time);
}
```

Then we can use our curry function to wrap our setTimeout to a 10-millisecond delay:

```
const delayTenMs = curry(setTimeoutWrapper)(10)
delayTenMs(() => console.log("Do X task"))
delayTenMs(() => console.log("Do Y task"))
```

which will work as we needed it to. The problem is, though, we must create wrappers like setTimeoutWrapper, which will be an overhead. That's where we can use *partial application* techniques.

Implementing **partial** Function

To fully understand how the partial application technique is working, we will be creating our own partial function in this section. Once the implementation is done, we will learn how to use our partial function with a simple example.

The implementation of the partial function looks like Listing 6-12.

Listing 6-12. partial Function Definition

```
const partial = function (fn,...partialArgs){
  let args = partialArgs;
  return function(...fullArguments) {
    let arg = 0;
    for (let i = 0; i < args.length && arg < fullArguments.
    length; i++) {
      if (args[i] === undefined) {
        args[i] = fullArguments[arg++];
        }
      }
      return fn.apply(null, args);
  };
};
```

Let's quickly use the partial function with our current problem:

```
let delayTenMs = partial(setTimeout,undefined,10);
delayTenMs(() => console.log("Do Y task"))
```

which will print to the console as you expect. Now let's walk through the implementation details of the partial function. Using closures, we are capturing the arguments that are passed to the function for the first time:

```
partial(setTimeout,undefined,10)

//will lead to
let args = partialArgs
=> args = [undefined,10]
```

We return a function that will remember the args value (yes, we are using closures again). The returned function is very easy. It takes an argument called fullArguments, so we call functions like delayTenMs by passing this argument:

```
delayTenMs(() => console.log("Do Y task"))

//fullArguments points to
//[() => console.log("Do Y task")]

//args using closures will have
//args = [undefined,10]
```

Now in the for loop we iterate and create the necessary arguments array for our function:

```
if (args[i] === undefined) {
    args[i] = fullArguments[arg++];
  }
}
```

Now let's start with value i as 0:

```
//args = [undefined,10]
//fullArguments = [() => console.log("Do Y task")]
args[0] => undefined === undefined //true
```

```
//inside if loop
args[0] = fullArguments[0]
=> args[0] = () => console.log("Do Y task")

//thus args will become
=> [() => console.log("Do Y task"),10]
```

As you can see in those code snippet examples, our args point to the array as we would expect for setTimeout function calls. Once we have the necessary arguments in args, we call the function via fn.apply(null, args).

Remember that we can apply partial for any function that has *n* arguments. To make the point concrete, let's look at an example. In JavaScript we use the following function call to do JSON pretty print:

```
let obj = {foo: "bar", bar: "foo"}
JSON.stringify(obj, null, 2);
```

As you can see, the last two arguments for the function called stringify are always going to be the same: null,2. We can use partial to remove the boilerplate:

```
let prettyPrintJson = partial(JSON.stringify,undefined,null,2)
```

You can then use prettyPrintJson to print the JSON:

```
prettyPrintJson({foo: "bar", bar: "foo"})
```

which will give you this output:

```
"{
  "foo": "bar",
  "bar": "foo"
}"
```

Note   There is a slight bug in our implementation of the `partial` function. What if you call `prettyPrintJson` again with a different argument? Does it work?

It always gives the result for the first invoked argument, but why? Can you see where we are making the mistake?

Hint: Remember, we are modifying the `partialArgs` by replacing the `undefined` values with our argument, and `Arrays` are used for reference.

Currying vs. Partial Application

We have seen both techniques, so the question is when to use which one. The answer depends on how your API is defined. If your API is defined as map,`filter`, then we can easily use the `curry` function to solve our problem. As discussed in the previous section, though, life is not always easy. There could be functions that are not designed for `curry` such as `setTimeout` in our examples. In those cases, the best option would be to use `partial` functions. After all, we use `curry` or `partial` to make function arguments and function setup easy and more powerful.

It's also important to note that currying will return nested unary functions; we have implemented `curry` so that it takes n arguments just for our convenience. It's also a proven fact that developers need either `curry` or `partial` but not both.

Summary

Currying and partial application are always a tool in functional programming. We started the chapter by explaining the definition of currying, which is nothing but converting a function of n arguments into nested unary functions. We saw the examples of currying and where it can be very useful, but there are cases where you want to fill the first two arguments of a function and the last argument, leaving the middle argument unknown for a certain time. That's where partial application comes into the picture. To fully understand both these concepts, we have implemented our own `curry` and `partial` functions. We have made a lot of progress, but we're not done yet.

Functional programming is all about composing functions, namely composing several small functions to build a new function. Composing and pipelines are the topics of the next chapter.

CHAPTER 7

Composition and Pipelines

In the previous chapter we saw two important techniques for functional programming: currying and partial application. We discussed how these two techniques work and that as JavaScript programmers we choose either currying or partial application in our code base. In this chapter we are going to see what functional composition means and its practical use cases.

Functional composition is simply referred to as *composition* in the functional programming world. We are going to see a bit of theory on the idea of composition and quite a few examples of it, then we will write our own compose function. Understanding how the compose function can be used to writer cleaner JavaScript is a fun task.

Note The chapter examples and library source code are in branch chap07. The repo's URL is https://github.com/antsmartian/functional-es8.git.

Once you check out the code, please check out branch chap07:

...

```
git checkout -b chap07 origin/chap07
```

...

© Anto Aravinth, Srikanth Machiraju 2018
A. Aravinth and S. Machiraju, *Beginning Functional JavaScript*,
https://doi.org/10.1007/978-1-4842-4087-8_7

For running the codes, as before run:

...

```
npm run playground
```

...

Composition in General Terms

Before we see what functional composition is all about, let's step back and understand the idea behind composition. In this section we explore the idea of composition by using a philosophy that is much more pronounced in the Unix world.

Unix Philosophy

Unix philosophy is a set of ideas that were originated by Ken Thompson. One part of the Unix philosophy is this:

> Make each program do one thing well. To do a
> new job, build afresh rather than complicate old
> programs by adding new "features."

This is exactly what we are doing as part of creating our functions. Functions, as we have seen until now in this book, are supposed to take an argument and return data. Yes, functional programming does follow Unix philosophy.

The second part of the philosophy is this:

> Expect the output of every program to become the
> input to another, as yet unknown, program.

That's an interesting quote. What does it mean by "Expect the output of every program to become the input to another"? To make the point clear, let's look at a few commands on a Unix platform that were built by following these philosophies.

For example, `cat` is a command (or you can think of it as a function) that is used to display the contents of a text file to a console. Here the `cat` command takes an argument (as similar to a function), that is, the file location, and so on, and returns the output (again as similar to a function) to the console. So we can do the following:

```
cat test.txt
```

which will print to the console

```
Hello world
```

Note   Here the content of `test.txt` will be `Hello world`.

That's so simple. Another command called `grep` allows us to search for content in a given text. An important point to note is that the `grep` function takes an input and gives the output (again very similar to a function).

We can do the following with the `grep` command:

```
grep 'world' test.txt
```

which will return the matching content, in this case:

```
Hello world
```

We have seen two quite simple functions—`grep` and `cat`—that are built by following the Unix philosophy. Now we can take some time to understand this quote:

> Expect the output of every program to become the input to another, as yet unknown, program.

Imagine you to want to send the data from the `cat` command as an input to the `grep` command to do a search. We know that the `cat` command will return the data; we also know that the `grep` command takes the data for processing the search operation. Thus, using the Unix | (pipe symbol), we can achieve our task:

```
cat test.txt | grep 'world'
```

which will return the data as expected:

```
Hello world
```

Note   The symbol | is called a pipe symbol. This allows us to combine several functions to create a new function that will help us to solve our problem. Basically | sends the output of a function on the left side as an input to a function on the right side! This process, technically, is called s pipeline.

This example might be trivial, but it conveys the idea behind the quote:

> Expect the output of every program to become the
> input to another, as yet unknown, program.

As our example shows, the `grep` command or a function receives the output of a `cat` command or a function. Here we have created a new function altogether without any effort by combining two existing base functions. Of course, here the | pipe acts as a *bridge* to connect the given two commands.

Let's change our problem statement a bit. What if we want to count the number of occurrences of the word *world* in a given text file? How we can achieve it?

This is how we are going to solve it:

```
cat test.txt | grep 'world' | wc
```

Note   The command wc is used to count the words in a given text. This command is available on all Unix and Linux platforms.

This is going to return the data as we expected. As the preceding examples show, we are creating a new function as per our need on the fly from our *base* functions! In other words, we are *composing* a new function from our base function(s). Note that the *base* function needs to obey this rule:

> Each base function needs to take an argument and
> return value.

We would be able to compose a new function with the help of |. As this chapter shows, we will be building our own compose function in JavaScript, which does the same job of | in the Unix and Linux world.

Now we have the idea of composing functions from base functions. The real advantage of composing functions is that we can combine our base function to solve the problem at hand, without re-creating a new function.

Functional Composition

In this section we discuss a use case where functional composition will be useful in the JavaScript world. Stay with us; you're going to absolutely love the idea of the compose function.

Revisiting map,filter

In Chapter 5, we saw how to chain the data from a map and filter to solve the problem at hand. Let's quickly revisit the problem and the solution.

We had an array of objects, the structure of which looks like Listing 7-1.

Listing 7-1. Apressbook Object Structure, Let `apressBooks` = [

```
    {
        "id": 111,
        "title": "C# 6.0",
        "author": "ANDREW TROELSEN",
        "rating": [4.7],
        "reviews": [{good : 4 , excellent : 12}]
    },
    {

        "id": 222,
        "title": "Efficient Learning Machines",
        "author": "Rahul Khanna",
        "rating": [4.5],
        "reviews": []
    },
    {

        "id": 333,
        "title": "Pro AngularJS",
        "author": "Adam Freeman",
        "rating": [4.0],
        "reviews": []
    },
    {

        "id": 444,
        "title": "Pro ASP.NET",
        "author": "Adam Freeman",
        "rating": [4.2],
        "reviews": [{good : 14 , excellent : 12}]
    }
];
```

The problem was to get the `title` and `author` objects out of `apressBooks` for which the review value is greater than `4.5`. Our solution to the problem was Listing 7-2.

Listing 7-2. Getting author Details Using map

```
map(filter(apressBooks, (book) => book.rating[0] > 4.5),
(book) => {
    return {title: book.title,author:book.author}
})
```

For this, the result is the following:

```
[
    {
            title: 'C# 6.0',
            author: 'ANDREW TROELSEN'
    }
]
```

The code to achieve the solution tells an important point. The data from our `filter` function is passed into the map function as its input argument. Yes, you have guessed it correctly: Does it sound like the same problem we solved in the previous section using | in the Unix world? Can we do the same thing in the JavaScript world? Can we create a function that will combine two functions by sending the output of one function as an input to another function? Yes, we can! Meet the `compose` function.

compose Function

In this section, let's create our first `compose` function. Creating a new `compose` function is easy and straightforward. The `compose` function needs to take the output of one function and provide it as input to another function. Let's write a simple `compose` function in Listing 7-3.

Listing 7-3. compose Function Definition

```
const compose = (a, b) =>
  (c) => a(b(c))
```

The compose function is simple and does what we need it to do. It takes two functions, a and b, and returns a function that takes one argument c. When we call the compose function by supplying the value of c, it will call the function b with input of c and the output of the function b goes into function a as input. That's exactly what a compose function definition is.

Now let's quickly test our compose function with a simple example before we dive into our running example from the previous section.

Note   The compose function executes b first and passes the return value of b as an argument to the function a. The direction of functions invoked in compose is right to left (i.e., b executes first, followed by a).

Playing with the **compose** Function

With our compose function in place, let's build some examples.

Imagine we want to round a given number. The number will be a float, so we have to convert that number to a float and then call Math.round.

Without compose, we can do the following:

```
let data = parseFloat("3.56")
let number = Math.round(data)
```

The output will be 4 as we would expect. As you can see in this example, the data (which is the output of the parseFloat function) is passed as input to Math.round to get a solution; this is the right problem candidate that our compose function will solve.

Let's solve this via our compose function:

```
let number = compose(Math.round,parseFloat)
```

This statement will return a new function that is stored as a number and looks like this:

```
number = (c) => Math.round(parseFloat(c))
```

Now if we pass the input c to our number function, we will get what we expect:

```
number("3.56")
=> 4
```

What we have just done is functional composition! Yes, we have composed two functions to build a new function on the fly! A key point to note here is that the functions Math.round and parseFloat aren't executed or run until we call our number function.

Now imagine we have two functions:

```
let splitIntoSpaces = (str) => str.split(" ");
let count = (array) => array.length;
```

Now if you want to build a new function to count the number of words in a string, we can easily do this:

```
const countWords = compose(count,splitIntoSpaces);
```

Now we can call that:

```
countWords("hello your reading about composition")
=> 5
```

The newly created function countWords using compose is an elegant and easy way to author simple functions by composing multiple base functions.

curry and partial to the Rescue

We know that we can compose two functions only if this function takes one input argument. That's not always the case, though, as there can be functions that have multiple arguments. How are we going to compose those functions? Is there something we can do about it?

Yes, we can do it using either the curry or partial functions that we defined in the previous chapter. Earlier in this chapter we used the following code to solve one of the problems (Listing 7-2):

```
map(filter(apressBooks, (book) => book.rating[0] > 4.5),
(book) => {
    return {title: book.title,author:book.author}
})
```

Now can we use the compose function to compose both map and filter with specifics to our example? Remember that both map and filter functions take two arguments: The first argument is the array and the second argument is the function to operate on that array. Therefore we cannot compose these two functions directly.

We can, however, take help from partial functions. Remember that the preceding code snippet does work on the apressBooks object. We pull it out here again for easy reference:

```
let apressBooks = [
    {
        "id": 111,
        "title": "C# 6.0",
        "author": "ANDREW TROELSEN",
        "rating": [4.7],
        "reviews": [{good : 4 , excellent : 12}]
    },
```

```
    {
        "id": 222,
        "title": "Efficient Learning Machines",
        "author": "Rahul Khanna",
        "rating": [4.5],
        "reviews": []
    },
    {

        "id": 333,
        "title": "Pro AngularJS",
        "author": "Adam Freeman",
        "rating": [4.0],
        "reviews": []
    },
    {

        "id": 444,
        "title": "Pro ASP.NET",
        "author": "Adam Freeman",
        "rating": [4.2],
        "reviews": [{good : 14 , excellent : 12}]
    }
];
```

Now let's say we have many small functions in our code base for filtering the books based on different ratings like the following:

```
let filterOutStandingBooks = (book) => book.rating[0] === 5;
let filterGoodBooks = (book) => book.rating[0] > 4.5;
let filterBadBooks = (book) => book.rating[0] < 3.5;
```

and we do have many projection functions like this:

```
let projectTitleAndAuthor = (book) => { return {title: book.
title,author:book.author} }
let projectAuthor = (book) => { return {author:book.author}  }
let projectTitle = (book) => { return {title: book.title} }
```

Note   You might be wondering why we have small functions even
for simple things. Remember that composition is all about small
functions being composed into a larger function. Simple functions are
easy to read, test, and maintain; and using compose we can build
anything out of it, as we will see in this section.

Now to solve our problem—to get book titles and authors with ratings
higher than 4.5—we can use compose and partial as in the following:

```
let queryGoodBooks = partial(filter,undefined,filterGoodBooks);
let mapTitleAndAuthor = partial(map,undefined,projectTitleAnd
Author)
```

```
let titleAndAuthorForGoodBooks = compose(mapTitleAndAuthor,
queryGoodBooks)
```

Let's take some time to understand the position of the partial
function in the current problem domain. As mentioned, the compose
function can only compose a function that takes one argument. However,
both filter and map take two arguments, so we cannot compose them
directly.

That's the reason we have used the partial function to partially apply
the second argument for both map and filter, as you can see here:

```
partial(filter,undefined,filterGoodBooks);
partial(map,undefined,projectTitleAndAuthor)
```

Here we have passed the filterGoodBooks function to query the books that have ratings over 4.5 and the projectTitleAndAuthor function to take the title and author properties from the apressBooks object. Now the returned partial application will expect only one argument, which is nothing but the array itself. With these two partial functions in place, we can compose them via compose as we already have done, as shown in Listing 7-4.

Listing 7-4. Using compose Function

```
let titleAndAuthorForGoodBooks = compose(mapTitleAndAuthor,
queryGoodBooks)
```

Now the function titleAndAuthorForGoodBooks expects one argument, in our case apressBooks; let's pass the object array to it:

```
titleAndAuthorForGoodBooks(apressBooks)
=> [
        {
                title: 'C# 6.0',
                author: 'ANDREW TROELSEN'
        }
]
```

We got back exactly what we wanted without compose, but the latest composed version titleAndAuthorForGoodBooks is much more readable and elegant in our opinion. You can sense the importance of creating small units of function that can be rebuilt using compose as per our needs.

In the same example, what if we want to get only the titles of the books with a rating higher than 4.5? It's simple:

```
let mapTitle = partial(map,undefined,projectTitle)
let titleForGoodBooks = compose(mapTitle,queryGoodBooks)
```

145

```
//call it
titleForGoodBooks(apressBooks)
=> [
        {
                title: 'C# 6.0'
        }
]
```

How about getting only author names for books with ratings that equal 5? That should be easy, right? We leave it to you to solve this using the functions already defined and the compose function.

Note   In this section, we have used partial to fill the arguments of a function. However you can use curry to do the same thing. It's just a matter of choice. Can you come up with a solution for using curry in our example here? (Hint: Reverse the order of argument for map, filter).

---

compose Many Functions

Currently our version of the compose function only composes two given functions. How about composing three, four, or n number of functions? Sadly, our current implementation doesn't handle this. Let's rewrite our compose function so that it can compose multiple functions on the fly.

Remember that we need to send the output of each function as an input to another function (by remembering the last executed function output recursively). We can use the reduce function, which we used in previous chapters to reduce the n of function calls one at a time. The rewritten compose function now looks like Listing 7-5.

Listing 7-5. compose many Function

```
const compose = (...fns) =>
  (value) =>
    reduce(fns.reverse(),(acc, fn) => fn(acc), value);
```

Note   This function is called composeN in the source code repo.

The important line of the function is this:

```
reduce(fns.reverse(),(acc, fn) => fn(acc), value);
```

Note   Recall from the previous chapter that we used the reduce function to reduce the array into a single value (along with an accumulator value; i.e., the third parameter of reduce). For example, to find the sum of the given array, using reduce:

```
reduce([1,2,3],(acc,it) => it + acc,0)=> 6
```

Here the array [1,2,3] is reduced into [6]; the accumulator value here is 0.

Here we are first reversing the function array via fns.reverse() and passing the function as (acc, fn) => fn(acc), which is going to call each function one after the other by passing the acc value as its argument. Notably, the initial accumulator value is nothing but a value variable, which will be the first input to our function.

With the new compose function in place, let's test it with our old example. In the previous section we composed a function to count words given in a string:

```
let splitIntoSpaces = (str) => str.split(" ");
let count = (array) => array.length;
const countWords = compose(count,splitIntoSpaces);
```

```
//count the words
countWords("hello your reading about composition")
=> 5
```

Imagine we want to find out whether the word count in the given string is odd or even. We already have a function for it:

```
let oddOrEven = (ip) => ip % 2 == 0 ? "even" : "odd"
```

Now with our compose function in place, we can compose these three functions to get what we really want:

```
const oddOrEvenWords = composeN(oddOrEven,count,splitIntoSpaces);
oddOrEvenWords("hello your reading about composition")
=> ["odd"]
```

We got back the expected result. Go and play around with our new compose function!

Now we have a solid understanding of how to use the compose function to get what we need. In the next section, we are going to see the same concept of compose in a different way, called *pipelines.*

Pipelines and Sequence

In the previous section, we saw that the data flow of compose is from left to right, as the functions on the left mostly get executed first, passing on the data to the next function, and so on, until the rightmost function gets executed last.

Certain people prefer the other way—where the rightmost function gets executed first and the leftmost function gets executed last. As you can remember, the data flow on Unix commands when we do | is from right to left. In this section, we are going to implement a new function called pipe that does exactly the same thing as the compose function, but just swaps the data flow.

Note   This process of flowing the data from right to left is called pipelines or even sequences. You can call them either pipeline or sequences as you prefer.

Implementing `pipe`

The `pipe` function is just a replica of our `compose` function; the only change is the data flow, as shown in Listing 7-6.

Listing 7-6. pipe Function Definition

```
const pipe = (...fns) =>
  (value) =>
    reduce(fns,(acc, fn) => fn(acc), value);
```

That's it. Note that there is no more call on `fns reverse` functions as in `compose`, which means we are going to execute the function order as it is (from left to right).

Let's quickly check our implementation of the `pipe` function by rerunning the same example as in the previous section:

```
const oddOrEvenWords = pipe(splitIntoSpaces,count,oddOrEven);
oddOrEvenWords("hello your reading about composition");
=> ["odd"]
```

The result is going to be the exact same; however, notice that we have changed the order of functions when we do piping. First, we call `splitIntoSpaces` and then `count` and finally `oddOrEven`.

Some people (who have knowledge of shell scripting) prefer pipes over `compose`. It's just a personal preference and nothing to do with the underlying implementation. The takeaway is that both `pipe` and `compose` do the same thing, but with different data flow. You can use either `pipe` or `compose` in your code base, but not both, as it can lead to confusion among your team members. Stick to one style of composing.

149

Odds on Composition

In this section, we discuss two topics. The first is one of the most important properties of compose: *Composition is associative*. The second discussion is on how we debug when we compose many functions.

Let's tackle one after the other.

Composition Is Associative

Functional composition is always associative. In general, the associative law states the outcome of the expression remains the same irrespective of the order of the parentheses, for example:

x * (y * z) = (x * y) * z = xyz

Likewise,

```
compose(f, compose(g, h)) == compose(compose(f, g), h);
```

Let's quickly check our previous section example:

```
//compose(compose(f, g), h)

let oddOrEvenWords = compose(compose(oddOrEven,count),splitInto
Spaces);
let oddOrEvenWords("hello your reading about composition")
=> ['odd']

//compose(f, compose(g, h))

let oddOrEvenWords = compose(oddOrEven,compose(count,splitIntoS
paces));
let oddOrEvenWords("hello your reading about composition")
=> ['odd']
```

As you can see in these examples, the result is going to be the same for both cases. Thus it proves the functional composition is associative. You might be wondering what the benefit of compose being associative is?

The real benefit is that it allows us to group functions into their own compose; that is:

```
let countWords = compose(count,splitIntoSpaces)
let oddOrEvenWords = compose(oddOrEven,countWords)
```

or

```
let countOddOrEven = compose(oddOrEven,count)
let oddOrEvenWords = compose(countOddOrEven,splitIntoSpaces)
```

or

...

This code is possible just because the composition possesses the associative property. Earlier in the chapter we discussed that creating small functions is the key to composing. Because compose is associative we can create small functions by composition, without any worry, as the result is going to be the same.

The Pipeline Operator

One other way of composing or chaining base functions is by using the pipeline operator. The pipeline operator is like the Unix pipe operator we saw earlier. The new pipeline operator is intended to make the chained JavaScript functions' code more readable and extendible.

Note   At the time of writing, the pipeline operator is still at Stage 1 draft (proposal) state in the TC39 approval workflow, which means it is not part of the ECMAScript specification yet. The latest status of this proposal along with browser compatibility will be available at https://github.com/tc39/proposals.

Let us see some examples of the pipeline operator.

Consider the following mathematical functions that operate on a single string argument.

```
const double = (n) => n * 2;
const increment = (n) => n + 1;
const ntimes = (n) => n * n;
```

Now, to call these functions on any number, normally we would write the following statement:

```
ntimes(double(increment(double(double(5)))));
```

This statement should return a value of 1764. The problem with this statement is the readability, as the sequence of operations or number of the operations is not readable. Linux-like systems use a pipeline operator like the one we saw at the beginning of the chapter. To make the code more readable a similar operator is being added to the ECMAScript 2017 (ECMA8). The name of the operator is pipeline (or binary infix operator), which looks like '|>'. The binary infix operator evaluates its left-hand side (LHS) and applies the right-hand side (RHS) to the LHS's value as a unary function call. Using this operator, the preceding statement can be written as shown here.

```
5 |> double |> double |> increment |> double |> ntimes    //
returns 1764.
```

That is more readable, isn't it? Of course, it is easier to read than the nested expressions, contains fewer or no parentheses, and has less indentation. Remember at this point it only works on unary functions, functions with only one argument.

Note   We haven't had the chance to execute it using the Babel compiler at the time of writing because the operator is in proposal state. You can try the preceding example when the proposal passes Stage 0 (Released) using the latest Babel compiler. You can also use an online Babel compiler like the one at `https://babeljs.io/`. The latest status of this proposal's inclusion into ECMAScript can be watched at `http://tc39.github.io/proposal-pipeline-operator/`.

Using the pipeline operator with our earlier example of getting the title and author of highly reviewed books is shown here.

```
let queryGoodBooks = partial(filter,undefined,filterGoodBooks);
let mapTitleAndAuthor = partial(map,undefined,projectTitleAnd
Author)
let titleAndAuthorForGoodBooks = compose(mapTitleAndAuthor,
queryGoodBooks)
titleAndAuthorForGoodBooks(apressBooks)
```

This can be rewritten more understandably as

```
apressBooks |> queryGoodBooks |>  mapTitleAndAuthor.
```

Once again, this operator just a syntactic alternative; the code behind the curtains remains the same, so it is a matter of choice for the developer. However, this pattern saves a few keystrokes by eliminating the effort to name intermediate variables. The GitHub repository for this pipeline operator is `https://github.com/babel/babel/tree/master/packages/babel-plugin-syntax-pipeline-operator`.

Although the pipeline operator works only on unary functions, there is a way around that to use it for functions with multiple arguments. Say we have these functions:

```
let add = (x, y) => x + y;
let double = (x) => x + x;

// without pipe operator
add(10, double(7))

// with pipe operator
7 |> double |> ( _=> add(10, _ )   // returns 24.
```

Note   Here the character _ can be replaced with any valid variable name.

Debugging Using the **tap** Function

We have used the compose function quite a lot in this chapter. The compose function can compose any number of functions. The data are going to flow from left to right in a chain until the full function list is evaluated. In this section, we teach you a trick that allows you to debug the failures on compose.

Let's create a simple function called identity. The aim of this function is to take the argument and return the same argument; hence the name *identity*.

```
const identity = (it) => {
        console.log(it);
        return it
}
```

Here we have added a simple `console.log` to print the value this function receives and also return it as it is. Now imagine we have the following call:

```
compose(oddOrEven,count,splitIntoSpaces)("Test string");
```

When you execute this code, what if the `count` function throws an error? How will you know what value the `count` function receives as its argument? That's where our little `identity` function comes into the picture. We can add `identity` in the flow where we see an error like this:

```
compose(oddOrEven,count,identity,splitIntoSpaces)("Test string");
```

That is going to print the input argument that the `count` function is going to receive. This simple function can be very helpful in debugging what data a function does receive.

Summary

We started this chapter by taking Unix philosophy as an example. We have seen how, by following the Unix philosophy, Unix commands like `cat`, `grep`, and `wc` could be able to compose as needed. We created our own version of the `compose` function to achieve the same in the JavaScript world. The simple `compose` function is useful to developers as we can compose complex functions as needed from our well-defined small functions. We also saw an example of how currying helps in functional composition, by a `partial` function.

We also discussed another function called `pipe`, which does exactly the same thing but inverts the data flow when compared to the `compose` function. At the end of the chapter we discussed an important property of `compose`: Composition is associative. We also introduced the usage of a new pipeline operator (|>) also called the binary infix operator, which can be used with unary functions. The pipeline operator is a proposal to ECMAScript 2017 that is at the proposal stage and will be available soon in the next release of ECMAScript. We also presented a small function called `identity` that we can use as our debugging tool while facing problems with the `compose` function.

In the next chapter, we are going to cover functors. Functors are very simple, but very powerful. We introduce use cases and a lot more about functors in the next chapter.

CHAPTER 8

Fun with Functors

In our previous chapter, we dealt with many functional programming techniques. In this chapter we are going to see yet another important concept in programming called *error handling*. Error handling is a common programming technique for handling errors in your application. The functional programming method of error handling will be different, though, and that's exactly what we are going to see in this chapter.

We will be looking at a new concept called *functor*. This new friend is going to help us handle errors in a purely functional way. Once we grasp the idea of a functor, we are going to implement two real-world functors: MayBe and Either. Let's get started.

Note The chapter examples and library source code are in branch chap08. The repo's URL is https://github.com/antsmartian/functional-es8.git.

Once you check out the code, please check out branch chap08:

...

```
git checkout -b chap08 origin/chap08
```

...

The original version of this chapter was revised. A correction to this chapter is available at https://doi.org/110.1007/978-1-4842-4087-8_13

© Anto Aravinth, Srikanth Machiraju 2018
A. Aravinth and S. Machiraju, *Beginning Functional JavaScript*,
https://doi.org/10.1007/978-1-4842-4087-8_8

For running the codes, as before run:

...

```
npm run playground
```

...

What Is a Functor?

In this section we are going to see what a functor really is. Here is its definition:

> A functor is a plain object (or type class in other
> languages) that implements the function map
> that, while running over each value in the object,
> produces a new object.

It is not that easy to understand the definition at first sight. We are going to break it down step by step so that we clearly understand it and see in action (via writing code) what a functor is.

Functor Is a Container

Simply put, a functor is a container that holds the value in it. We have seen this in the definition stating that functor is a plain object. Let's create a simple container that can hold any value we pass into it, and call it a Container (see Listing 8-1).

Listing 8-1. Container Definition

```
const Container = function(val) {
        this.value = val;
}
```

Note   You might be wondering why we didn't write the `Container`
function using our arrow syntax:

```
const Container = (val) => {

this.value = val;

}
```

That code will be fine, but the moment we try to apply the `new`
keyword on our `Container`, we will get an error like this:

```
Container is not a constructor(...)(anonymous
function)
```

Why is that? Well, technically, to create a new `Object`, the function
should have the internal method `[[Construct]]` and the property
prototype. Sadly, the `Arrow` function doesn't have both! So here we
are falling back to our old friend `function`, which has the internal
method `[[Construct]]`, and it also has access to the prototype
property.

Now with `Container` in place, we can create a new object out of it, as
shown in Listing 8-2.

Listing 8-2. Playing With Container

```
let testValue = new Container(3)
=> Container(value:3)

let testObj = new Container({a:1})
=> Container(value:{a:1})

let testArray = new Container([1,2])
=> Container(value:[1,2])
```

Container is just holding the value inside it. We can pass any data type in JavaScript to it and Container will hold it. Before we move on, we can create a util method called of in the Container prototype, which will save us in writing the new keyword to create a new Container. The code looks like Listing 8-3.

Listing 8-3. of Method Definition

```
Container.of = function(value) {
  return new Container(value);
}
```

With this of method in place, we can rewrite the code in Listing 8-2 as shown in Listing 8-4.

Listing 8-4. Creating Container with of

```
testValue = Container.of(3)
=> Container(value:3)

testObj = Container.of({a:1})
=> Container(value:{a:1})

testArray = new Container([1,2])
=> Container(value:[1,2])
```

It is worth noting that Container can contain nested Containers, too.

```
Container.of(Container.of(3));
```

is going to print:

```
Container {
      value: Container {
              value: 3
      }
}
```

Now that we have defined that the functor is nothing but a `Container` that can hold the value, let's revisit the definition of a functor.

Functor is a plain object (or type class in other languages) that implements the function map while running over each value in the object to produce a new object.

It looks like functor needs to implement a method called map. Let's implement that method in the next section.

Implementing map

Before we implement the map function, let's pause here and think about why we need the map function in the first place. Remember that we created `Container` that just holds the value we pass into it. Holding the value hardly has any use, though, and that is where the map function comes into place. The map function allows us to call any function on the value that is being currently held by the `Container`.

The map function takes the value out of the `Container`, applies the passed function on that value, and again puts the result back in the `Container`. Let's visualize using the image shown in Figure 8-1.

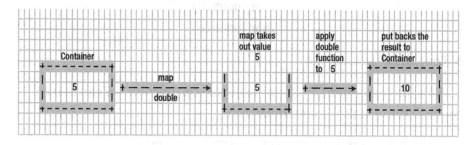

Figure 8-1. *Mechanism of Container and map function*

Figure 8-1 shows the way the map function is going to work with our `Container` object. It takes the value in the `Container`—in this case the value is 5—and passes on that value to the passed function double (this function just doubles the given number). The result is put back again into the `Container`. With that understanding in place, we can implement the map function, as shown in Listing 8-5.

Listing 8-5. map Function Definition

```
Container.prototype.map = function(fn){
  return Container.of(fn(this.value));
}
```

As shown earlier, the preceding map function simply does what we have discussed in Figure 8-1. It's simple and elegant. Now to make the point concrete, let's put our image piece into code action:

```
let double = (x) => x + x;
Container.of(3).map(double)
=> Container { value: 6 }
```

Note that the map returns the result of the passed function again in the container, which allows us to chain the operation:

```
Container.of(3).map(double)
                          .map(double)
                          .map(double)

=> Container {value: 24}
```

Now implementing `Container` with our map function, we can make complete sense of the functor definition:

> Functor is a plain object (or type class in other
> languages) that implements the function map
> that, while running over each value in the object,
> produces a new object.

Or in other words:

Functor is an object that implements a map contract.

Now that we have defined it, you might be wondering what functor is useful for. We are going to answer that in the next section.

Note   Functor is a *concept* that looks for a contract. The contract as we have seen is simple, implementing map. The way in which we implement the map function provides different types of functor like MayBe and Either, which we are going to discuss later in this chapter.

MayBe

We started the chapter with the argument of how we handle errors and exception using functional programming techniques. In the previous section we learned about the fundamental concept of functor. In this section, we are going to see a *type* of functor called MayBe. The MayBe functor allows us to handle errors in our code in a more functional way.

Implementing MayBe

MayBe is a type of functor, which means it's going to implement a map function but in a different way. Let's start with a simple MayBe in Listing 8-6, which can hold the data (very similar to a Container implementation):

Listing 8-6. MayBe Function Definition

```
const MayBe = function(val) {
  this.value = val;
}
MayBe.of = function(val) {
  return new MayBe(val);
}
```

We just created MayBe, which resembles the Container implementation. As stated earlier, we have to implement a map contract for the MayBe, which looks like Listing 8-7.

Listing 8-7. MayBe's map Function Definition

```
MayBe.prototype.isNothing = function() {
  return (this.value === null || this.value === undefined);
};
MayBe.prototype.map = function(fn) {
  return this.isNothing() ? MayBe.of(null) : MayBe.of(fn(this.
  value));
};
```

The map function does very similar things to the Container (simple functor) map function. MayBe's map first checks whether the value in the container is null or undefined before applying the passed function using the isNothing function, which takes care of null and undefined checks:

```
(this.value === null || this.value === undefined);
```

Note that map puts the result of applying the function back in the container:

```
return this.isNothing() ? Maybe.of(null) : Maybe.of(f(this.__
value));
```

Now it's time to see MayBe in action.

Simple Use Cases

As we discussed in the previous section, MayBe checks the null, undefined before applying the passed function in map. This is a very powerful abstraction that takes care of error handling. To make this concrete, a simple example is provided in Listing 8-8.

Listing 8-8. Creating our First MayBe

```
MayBe.of("string").map((x) => x.toUpperCase())
```

which returns

```
MayBe { value: 'STRING' }
```

The most important and interesting point to note here is this:

```
(x) => x.toUpperCase()
```

doesn't care if x is null or undefined or that it has been abstracted by the MayBe functor. What if the value of the string is null? Then the code looks like this:

```
MayBe.of(null).map((x) => x.toUpperCase())
```

We will be getting back this:

```
MayBe { value: null }
```

Now our code doesn't explode in null or undefined values as we have wrapped our value in the *type safety* container MayBe. We are now handling the null values in a declarative way.

Note   On MayBe.of(null) case, if we call the map function, from our implementation we know that map first checks if the value is null or undefined by calling isNothing:

```
//implementation of map

MayBe.prototype.map = function(fn) {

return this.isNothing() ? MayBe.of(null) : MayBe.of(fn(this.value));

};
```

if isNothing returns true. We return back MayBe.of(null) instead of calling the passed function.

In a normal imperative way, we would have done this:

```
let value = "string"
if(value != null || value != undefined)
        return value.toUpperCase();
```

The preceding code does exactly the same thing, but look at the steps required to check if the value is null or undefined, even for a single call. Also using MayBe, we don't care about those sneaky variables to hold the resulting value. Remember that we can chain our map function as desired, as shown in Listing 8-9.

Listing 8-9. Chaining with map

```
MayBe.of("George")
    .map((x) => x.toUpperCase())
    .map((x) => "Mr. " + x)
```

gives back:

```
MayBe { value: 'Mr. GEORGE' }
```

Before we close this section, we need to talk about two more important properties of MayBe. The first one is that even if your passed function to map returns null/undefined, MayBe can take care of it. In other words, in the whole chain of map calls, it is fine if a function returns null or undefined. To illustrate the point, let's tweak the last example:

```
MayBe.of("George")
    .map(() => undefined)
    .map((x) => "Mr. " + x)
```

Note that our second map function returns undefined; however, running the preceding code will give this result:

```
MayBe { value: null }
```

as expected.

The second important point is that all map functions will be called regardless if they receive null/undefined. We'll pull out the same code snippet (Listing 8-9) that we used in the previous example:

```
MayBe.of("George")
    .map(() => undefined)
    .map((x) => "Mr. " + x)
```

The point here is that even though the first map does return undefined:

```
map(() => undefined)
```

the second map will be called *always* (i.e., the chained maps to any level will be called always); it is just that the next map function in the chain returns undefined (as the previous map returns undefined/null), without applying the passed function. This process is repeated until the last map function call is evaluated in the chain.

Real-World Use Cases

Because MayBe is a type of container that can hold any values, it can also hold values of type Array. Imagine you have written an API to get the top 10 SubReddit data based on types like top, new, and hot (see Listing 8-10).

Listing 8-10. Getting Top 10 SubReddit Posts

```
let getTopTenSubRedditPosts = (type) => {
    let response
    try{
        response = JSON.parse(request('GET',"https://www.
        reddit.com/r/subreddits/" + type + ".json?limit=10").
        getBody('utf8'))
    }catch(err) {
        response = { message: "Something went wrong" ,
        errorCode: err['statusCode'] }
    }
    return response
}
```

Note   request comes from the package sync-request. This will allow us to fire a request and get the response in synchronous fashion. This is just for illustration; we don't recommend using synchronous calls in production.

The getTopTenSubRedditPosts function just hits the URL and gets the response. If there are any issues in hitting the Reddit API, it sends back a custom response of this format:

```
. . .
response = { message: "Something went wrong" , errorCode:
err['statusCode'] }
. . .
```

If we call our API like this:

```
getTopTenSubRedditPosts('new')
```

we will be getting back the response in this format:

```
{"kind": "Listing", "data": {"modhash": "", "children": [],
"after": null, "before": null}}
```

where the children property will have an array of JSON objects. It will look something like this:

```
"{
  "kind": "Listing",
  "data": {
    "modhash": "",
    "children": [
      {
        "kind": "t3",
        "data": {
          . . .
          "url": "https://twitter.com/malyw/
          status/780453672153124864",
          "title": "ES7 async/await landed in Chrome",
          . . .
        }
      }
    ],
    "after": "t3_54lnrd",
    "before": null
  }
}"
```

From the response we need to return the array of JSON object that has the `URL` and `title` in it. Remember that if we pass an invalid subreddit type such as `test` to our `getTopTenSubRedditPosts`, it will return an error response that does not have a `data` or `children` property.

With `MayBe` in place, we can go ahead and implement the logic as shown in Listing 8-11.

Listing 8-11. Getting Top 10 SubReddit Posts Using MayBe

```
//arrayUtils from our library
import {arrayUtils} from '../lib/es8-functional.js'

let getTopTenSubRedditData = (type) => {
    let response = getTopTenSubRedditPosts(type);
    return MayBe.of(response).map((arr) => arr['data'])
                         .map((arr) => arr['children'])
                         .map((arr) => arrayUtils.map(arr,
                            (x) => {
                                return {
                                    title : x['data'].
                                    title,
                                    url   : x['data'].url
                                }
                            }
                        ))
}
```

Let's break down how `getTopTenSubRedditData` works. First we are wrapping the result of the Reddit API call within the `MayBe` context using `MayBe.of(response)`. Then we are running a series of functions using `MayBe`'s map:

```
. . .
.map((arr) => arr['data'])
.map((arr) => arr['children'])
. . .
```

This will return the children array object from the response structure:

```
{"kind": "Listing", "data": {"modhash": "", "children":
[ . . . .], "after": null, "before": null}}
```

In the last map, we are using our own ArrayUtils's map to iterate over the children property and return only the title and URL as needed:

```
. . .
.map((arr) =>
        arrayUtils.map(arr,
    (x) => {
        return {
            title : x['data'].title,
            url   : x['data'].url
        }
    }
. . .
```

Now if we call our function with a valid Reddit name like new:

```
getTopTenSubRedditData('new')
```

we get back this response:

```
MayBe {
  value:
   [ { title: '/r/UpliftingKhabre - The subreddit for uplifting
   and positive stories from India!',
       url: 'https://www.reddit.com/r/ },
```

```
{ title: 'Angel Vivaldi channel',
  url: 'https://qa1web-portal.immerss.com/angel-vivaldi/
  angel-vivaldi' },
{ title: 'r/test12 - Come check us out for INSANE.',
  url: 'https://www.reddit.com/r/' },
{ title: 'r/Just - Come check us out for GREAT',
  url: 'https://www.reddit.com/r/just/' },
{ title: 'r/Just - Come check us out for GREAT',
  url: 'https://www.reddit.com/r/just/' },
{ title: 'How to Get Verified Facebook',
  url: 'http://imgur.com/VffRnGb' },
{ title: '/r/TrollyChromosomes - A support group for those
of us whose trollies or streetcars suffer from chronic
genetic disorders',
  url: 'https://www.reddit.com/r/trollychromosomes' },
{ title: 'Yemek Tarifleri Eskimeyen Tadlarımız',
  url: 'http://otantiktad.com/' },
{ title: '/r/gettoknowyou is the ultimate socializing
subreddit!',
  url: 'https://www.reddit.com/r/subreddits/
  comments/50wcju/rgettoknowyou_is_the_ultimate_
  socializing/' } ] }
```

Note   The response might not be the same for the readers, as the response will change from time to time.

The beauty of the getTopTenSubRedditData method is how it handles unexpected input that can cause null/undefined errors in our logic flow. What if someone calls your getTopTenSubRedditData with a wrong Reddit type? Remember that it will return the JSON response from Reddit:

```
{ message: "Something went wrong" , errorCode: 404 }
```

That is, the data—children property—will be empty. Try this by passing the wrong Reddit type and see how it responds:

```
getTopTenSubRedditData('new')
```

which returns:

```
MayBe { value: null }
```

without throwing any error. Even though our map function tries to get the data from the response (which is not present in this case), it returns MayBe.of(null), so the corresponding maps would not apply the passed function, as we discussed earlier.

We can clearly sense how MayBe handled all the undefined/null errors with ease. Our getTopTenSubRedditData looks so declarative.

That's all about the MayBe Functor. We are going to meet another functor in the next section called Either.

Either Functor

In this section we are going to create a new functor called Either, which will allow us to solve the branching-out problem. To provide a context, let's revisit an example from the previous section (Listing 8-9):

```
MayBe.of("George")
    .map(() => undefined)
    .map((x) => "Mr. " + x)
```

This code will return the result

```
MayBe {value: null}
```

as we would expect. However, the question is which branching (i.e., out of two earlier map calls) failed with undefined or null values. We cannot answer this question easily with MayBe. The only way is to manually dig into the branching of MayBe and discover the culprit. This doesn't mean that MayBe has flaws, but just that in certain use cases, we need a better functor than MayBe (mostly where you have many nested maps). This is where Either comes into the picture.

Implementing Either

We have seen the problem Either is going to solve for us; now let's see its implementation (Listing 8-12).

Listing 8-12. Either Functor Parts Definition

```
const Nothing = function(val) {
  this.value = val;
};

Nothing.of = function(val) {
  return new Nothing(val);
};

Nothing.prototype.map = function(f) {
  return this;
};

const Some = function(val) {
  this.value = val;
};
```

```
Some.of = function(val) {
  return new Some(val);
};

Some.prototype.map = function(fn) {
  return Some.of(fn(this.value));
}
```

The implementation has two functions, Some and Nothing. You can see that Some is just a copy of a Container with a name change. The interesting part is with Nothing. Nothing is also a Container, but its map doesn't run over a given function but rather just returns this:

```
Nothing.prototype.map = function(f) {
  return this;
};
```

In other words, you can run your functions on Some but not on Nothing (not a technical statement, right?). Here's a quick example:

```
Some.of("test").map((x) => x.toUpperCase())
=> Some {value: "TEST"}

Nothing.of("test").map((x) => x.toUpperCase())
=> Nothing {value: "test"}
```

As shown in the preceding code snippet, calling map on Some runs over the passed function. However, in Nothing, it just returns the same value, test. We wrap these two objects into the Either object as shown in Listing 8-13.

Listing 8-13. Either Definition

```
const Either = {
  Some : Some,
  Nothing: Nothing
}
```

You might be wondering what the usefulness of Some or Nothing are. To understand this, let's revisit our Reddit example version of MayBe.

Reddit Example **Either** Version

The MayBe version of the Reddit example looks like this (Listing 8-11):

```
let getTopTenSubRedditData = (type) => {
    let response = getTopTenSubRedditPosts(type);
    return MayBe.of(response).map((arr) => arr['data'])
                             .map((arr) => arr['children'])
                             .map((arr) => arrayUtils.map(arr,
                                (x) => {
                                    return {
                                        title : x['data'].
                                        title,
                                        url   : x['data'].url
                                    }
                                }
                             ))
}
```

On passing a wrong Reddit type, say, for example, unknown:

```
getTopTenSubRedditData('unknown')
=> MayBe {value : null}
```

we get back MayBe of null value, but we didn't know why null was returned. We know that getTopTenSubRedditData uses getTopTenSubRedditPosts to get the response. Now that Either is in place, we can create a new version of getTopTenSubRedditPosts using Either, as shown in Listing 8-14.

Listing 8-14. Get Top Ten Subreddit Using Either

```
let getTopTenSubRedditPostsEither = (type) => {

    let response
    try{
        response = Some.of(JSON.parse(request('GET',
        "https://www.reddit.com/r/subreddits/" + type +
        ".json?limit=10").getBody('utf8')))
    }catch(err) {          response = Nothing.of({ message:
    "Something went wrong" , errorCode: err['statusCode'] })
    }
    return response
}
```

Note that we have wrapped the proper response with Some and the error response with Nothing. Now with that in place, we can modify our Reddit API to the code shown in Listing 8-15.

Listing 8-15. Get Top Ten Subreddit Using Either

```
let getTopTenSubRedditDataEither = (type) => {
    let response = getTopTenSubRedditPostsEither(type);
    return response.map((arr) => arr['data'])
                   .map((arr) => arr['children'])
                   .map((arr) => arrayUtils.map(arr,
                     (x) => {
                         return {
                             title : x['data'].
                             title,
                             url   : x['data'].url
                         }
                     }
                 ))
}
```

This code is just literally the MayBe version, but it's just not using MayBe; rather it's using Either's type.

Now let's call our new API with the wrong Reddit data type:

```
getTopTenSubRedditDataEither('new2')
```

This will return

```
Nothing { value: { message: 'Something went wrong', errorCode: 404 } }
```

This is so brilliant. Now with Either types in place, we get back the exact reason why our branching failed. As you can guess, getTopTenSubRedditPostsEither returns Nothing in case of an error (i.e., unknown Reddit type); hence the mappings on getTopTenSubRedditDataEither will never happen because it is of type Nothing. You can sense how Nothing helped us in preserving the error message and also blocking the functions to map over.

On a closing note, we can try our new version with a valid Reddit type:

```
getTopTenSubRedditDataEither('new')
```

It will return the expected response in Some:

```
Some {
  value:
   [ { title: '/r/UpliftingKhabre - The subreddit for uplifting
   and positive stories from India!',
      url: 'https://www.reddit.com/r/ },
     { title: '/R/ - The Best Place To Off To Your Fave,
      url: 'https://www.reddit.com/r/ },
     { title: 'Angel Vivaldi channel',
      url: 'https://qa1web-portal.immerss.com/angel-vivaldi/
      angel-vivaldi' },
     { title: 'r/test12 - Come check us out for INSANE',
```

```
  url: 'https://www.reddit.com/r/ /' },
{ title: 'r/Just - Come check us out for',
  url: 'https://www.reddit.com/r/just/' },
{ title: 'r/Just - Come check us out for',
  url: 'https://www.reddit.com/r/' },
{ title: 'How to Get Verified Facebook',
  url: 'http://imgur.com/VffRnGb' },
{ title: '/r/TrollyChromosomes - A support group for those
of us whose trollies or streetcars suffer from chronic
genetic disorders',
  url: 'https://www.reddit.com/r/trollychromosomes' },
{ title: 'Yemek Tarifleri Eskimeyen Tadlarımız',
  url: 'http://otantiktad.com/' },
{ title: '/r/gettoknowyou is the ultimate socializing
subreddit!',
  url: 'https://www.reddit.com/r/subreddits/comments/50wcju/
  rgettoknowyou_is_the_ultimate_socializing/' } ] }
```

That's all about `Either`.

Note   If you are from a Java background, you can sense that
`Either` is very similar to `Optional` in Java 8. In fact, `Optional` is
a functor.

Word of Caution: Pointed Functor

Before we close the chapter, we need to make a point clear. In the
beginning of the chapter we started saying that we created the `of` method
just to escape the `new` keyword in place for creating `Container`. We did the
same for `MayBe` and `Either` as well. To recall, functor is just an interface
that has a `map` contract. *Pointed functor* is a subset of functor, which has an
interface that has an `of` contract.

What we have designed thus far is called a pointed functor. This is just to make the terms right in the book, but you got to see what problem functor or pointed functor solves for us in the real world, which is more important.

Summary

We started our chapter by asking questions about how we will be handling exceptions in the functional programming world. We began with creating a simple functor. We defined a functor as being nothing but a container with a map function implemented. Then we went ahead and implemented a functor called MayBe. We saw how MayBe helps us in avoiding pesky null/undefined checks. MayBe allowed us to write code in functional and declarative ways. Then we saw how Either helped us to preserve the error message while branching out. Either is just a supertype of Some and Nothing. Now we have seen functors in action.

CHAPTER 9

Monads in Depth

In the previous chapter we saw what functors are and how they are useful
to us. In this chapter we are going to continue with functors, learning about
a new functor called a monad. Don't be afraid of the terms; the concepts
are easy to understand.

We are going to start with a problem of retrieving and displaying
the Reddit comments for our search query. Initially we are going to use
functors, especially the MayBe functor, to solve this problem. As we solve
the problem, though, we are going to encounter a few issues with the MayBe
functor. Then we will be moving ahead to create a special type of functor
called a *monad*.

Note   The chapter examples and library source code are in branch
chap09. The repo's URL is https://github.com/antsmartian/
functional-es8.git

Once you check out the code, please check out branch chap09:

...

git checkout -b chap09 origin/chap09

...

© Anto Aravinth, Srikanth Machiraju 2018
A. Aravinth and S. Machiraju, *Beginning Functional JavaScript*,
https://doi.org/10.1007/978-1-4842-4087-8_9

For running the codes, as before run:

. . .

```
npm run playground
```

. . .

Getting Reddit Comments for Our Search Query

We have been using Reddit API starting with the previous chapter. In this section, we use the same Reddit API for searching the posts with our query and getting the list of comments for each of the search results. We are going to use MayBe for this problem; as we saw in the previous chapter, MayBe allows us to focus on the problem without worrying about null/undefined values.

Note   You might be wondering why we are not using the Either functor for the current problem, as MayBe has a few drawbacks of not capturing the error when branching out as we saw in the previous chapter. That's true, but the reason we have chosen MayBe is mainly to keep things simple. As you see, we will be extending the same idea to Either as well.

The Problem

Before we begin implementing the solution, let's look at the problem and its associated Reddit API endpoints. The problem contains two steps:

1. For searching specific posts and comments we need to hit the Reddit API endpoint:

   `https://www.reddit.com/search.json?q=<SEARCH_STRING>`

   and pass along the SEARCH_STRING. For example, if we search for the string functional programming like this:

   `https://www.reddit.com/search.json?q=`
   `functional%20programming`

   we get back the result shown in Listing 9-1.

Listing 9-1. Structure of Reddit Response

```
{ kind: 'Listing',
  data:
    { facets: {},
      modhash: ",
      children:
        [ [Object],
          [Object],
          [Object],
          [Object],
          [Object],
          [Object],

          . . .
```

```
        [Object],
        [Object] ],
     after: 't3_terth',
     before: null } }
```

and each children object looks like this:

```
{ kind: 't3',
  data:
   { contest_mode: false,
     banned_by: null,
     domain: 'self.compsci',
     . . .
     downs: 0,
     mod_reports: [],
     archived: true,
     media_embed: {},
     is_self: true,
     hide_score: false,
     permalink: '/r/compsci/comments/3mecup/eli5_what_is_
     functional_programming_and_how_is_it/?ref=search_posts',
     locked: false,
     stickied: false,
     . . .
     visited: false,
     num_reports: null,
     ups: 134 } }
```

These objects specify the results that are matching
our search query.

2. Once we have the search result, we need to get each
    search result's comments. How do we do that? As
    mentioned in the previous point, each children
    object is our search result. These objects have a field
    called permalink, which looks like this:

    ```
    permalink: '/r/compsci/comments/3mecup/eli5_what_is_
    functional_programming_and_how_is_it/?ref=search_posts',
    ```

    We need to navigate to the preceding URL:

```
GET: https://www.reddit.com//r/compsci/comments/3mecup/eli5_
what_is_functional_programming_and_how_is_it/.json
```

That is going to return the array of comments like the following:

```
[Object,Object,..,Object]
```

where each Object gives the information about comments.

Once we get the comments object, we need to merge the result with
title and return a new object:

```
{

    title : Functional programming in plain English,
    comments : [Object,Object,..,Object]

}
```

where title is the title we get from the first step. Now with our
understanding of the problem, let's implement the logic.

Implementation of the First Step

In this section, we implement the solution for the first step, which involves
firing a request to the Reddit search API endpoint along with our search
query. Because we need to fire the HTTP GET call, we will be requiring the
sync-request module that we used in the previous chapter.

Let's pull out the module and hold it in a variable for future use:

```
let request = require('sync-request');
```

Now with the request function, we could fire the HTTP GET call to our Reddit search API endpoint. Let's wrap the search steps in a specific function, which we call searchReddit (Listing 9-2).

Listing 9-2. searchReddit Function Definition

```
let searchReddit = (search) => {
    let response
    try{
        response = JSON.parse(request('GET',"https://www.reddit.
        com/search.json?q=" + encodeURI(search)).getBody('utf8'))
    }catch(err) {
        response = { message: "Something went wrong" ,
        errorCode: err['statusCode'] }
    }
    return response
}
```

Now we'll walk through the code in steps.

1. We are firing the search request to the URL endpoint
   https://www.reddit.com/search.json?q= as
   shown here:

   ```
   response = JSON.parse(request('GET',"https://www.
   reddit.com/search.json?q=" + encodeURI(search)).
   getBody('utf8'))
   ```

   Note that we are using the encodeURI method for
   escaping special characters in our search string.

2. Once the response is a success, we are returning
   back the value.

3. In case of error, we are catching it in a `catch` block
    and getting the error code and returning the error
    response like this:

```
. . .
catch(err) {
        response = { message: "Something went wrong" ,
        errorCode: err['statusCode'] }
    }
. . .
```

With our little function in place, we go ahead and test it:

```
searchReddit("Functional Programming")
```

This will return the following result:

```
{ kind: 'Listing',
  data:
    { facets: {},
      modhash: ",
      children:
        [ [Object],
          [Object],
          [Object],
          [Object],
          [Object],
          [Object],
          [Object],
          [Object],
          . . .
      after: 't3_terth',
      before: null } }
```

That's perfect. We are done with Step 1. Let's implement Step 2.

Implementing the second step for each search `children` object, we need to get its `permalink` value to get the list of comments. We can write a separate method for getting a list of comments for the given URL. We call this method `getComments`. The implementation of `getComments` is simple, as shown in Listing 9-3.

Listing 9-3. getComments Function Definition

```
let getComments = (link) => {
    let response
    try {
        response = JSON.parse(request('GET',"https://www.
        reddit.com/" + link).getBody('utf8'))
    } catch(err) {
        response = { message: "Something went wrong" ,
        errorCode: err['statusCode'] }
    }

    return response
}
```

The `getComments` implementation is very similar to our `searchReddit`. Let's walk through the steps and see what `getComments` does.

1. It fires the HTTP GET call for the given `link` value. For example, if the `link` value is passed as:

   `r/IAmA/comments/3wyb3m/we_are_the_team_working_on_react_native_ask_us/.json`

   `getComments` then will fire an HTTP GET call to the URL:

   `https://www.reddit.com/r/IAmA/comments/3wyb3m/we_are_the_team_working_on_react_native_ask_us/.json` which is going to return the array of comments. As before, we are a bit defensive here and catching any errors within the getComments method in our favorite catch block. Finally, we are returning back the response.

Quickly we'll test our getComments by passing the following link value:

r/IAmA/comments/3wyb3m/we_are_the_team_working_on_react_native_ ask_us/.json

```
getComments('r/IAmA/comments/3wyb3m/we_are_the_team_working_on_
react_native_ask_us/.json')
```

For this call we get back this result:

```
[ { kind: 'Listing',
    data: { modhash: ", children: [Object], after: null,
    before: null } },
  { kind: 'Listing',
    data: { modhash: ", children: [Object], after: null,
    before: null } } ]
```

Now with both APIs ready, it's time to merge these results.

Merging Reddit Calls

Now we have defined two functions, namely, searchReddit and getComments (Listing 9-2 and Listing 9-3, respectively), that perform their tasks and return the responses seen in the previous sections. In this section, let's write a higher level function, which takes up the search text and use these two functions to achieve our end goal.

We'll call the function we create mergeViaMayBe and its implementation looks like Listing 9-4.

Listing 9-4. mergeViaMayBe Function Definition

```
let mergeViaMayBe = (searchText) => {

    let redditMayBe = MayBe.of(searchReddit(searchText))
    let ans = redditMayBe
                .map((arr) => arr['data'])
                .map((arr) => arr['children'])
                .map((arr) => arrayUtils.map(arr, (x) => {
                        return {
                            title : x['data'].title,
                            permalink : x['data'].permalink
                        }
                    }
                ))
                .map((obj) => arrayUtils.map(obj, (x) => {
                    return {
                        title: x.title,
                        comments: MayBe.of(getComments(x.
                        permalink.replace("?ref=search_posts",".
                        json")))
                    }
                }));

    return ans;
}
```

Let's quickly check our function by passing the search text functional programming:

```
mergeViaMayBe('functional programming')
```

That call will give this result:

```
MayBe {
  value:
   [ { title: 'ELI5: what is functional programming and how is
   it different from OOP',
      comments: [Object] },
    { title: 'ELI5 why functional programming seems to be "on
    the rise" and how it differs from OOP',
      comments: [Object] } ] }
```

Note   For better clarity we have reduced the number of results in the output of this call. The default call will give back 25 results, which will take a couple of pages to put in the output of `mergeViaMayBe`. From here on, we display only minimal output in the book. Note, though, that the source code example does call and print all 25 results.

Now let's step back and understand in detail what the `mergeViaMayBe` function does. The function first calls the `searchReddit` with `searchText` value. The result of the call is wrapped in `MayBe`:

```
let redditMayBe = MayBe.of(searchReddit(searchText))
```

Once the result is wrapped inside a `MayBe` type, we are free to map over it as you can see in the code.

To remind us of the search query (which our `searchReddit` will call), it will send back the result in the following structure:

```
{ kind: 'Listing',
  data:
   { facets: {},
     modhash: ",
```

```
children:
 [ [Object],
   [Object],
   [Object],
   [Object],
   [Object],
   [Object],
   . . .
   [Object],
   [Object] ],
  after: 't3_terth',
  before: null } }
```

To get the permalink (which is in our children object), we need to navigate to data.children. This is demonstrated in the code:

```
redditMayBe
        .map((arr) => arr['data'])
        .map((arr) => arr['children'])
```

Now that we have a handle on a children array, remember that each children has an object with the following structure:

```
{ kind: 't3',
  data:
   { contest_mode: false,
     banned_by: null,
     domain: 'self.compsci',
     . . .
     permalink: '/r/compsci/comments/3mecup/eli5_what_is_
     functional_programming_and_how_is_it/?ref=search_posts',
     locked: false,
     stickied: false,
     . . .
```

```
visited: false,
num_reports: null,
ups: 134 } }
```

We need to get only `title` and `permalink` out of it; because it's an array, we run `Array`'s `map` function over it:

```
.map((arr) => arrayUtils.map(arr, (x) => {
    return {
        title : x['data'].title,
        permalink : x['data'].permalink
    }
  }
))
```

Now that we have both `title` and `permalink`, our last step is to take `permalink` and pass it to our `getComments` function, which will fetch the list of comments for the passed value. This is seen here in the code:

```
.map((obj) => arrayUtils.map(obj, (x) => {
    return {
        title: x.title,
        comments: MayBe.of(getComments(x.permalink.
        replace("?ref=search_posts",".json")))
    }
}));
```

Because the call of `getComments` can get an error value, we are wrapping it again inside a `MayBe`:

. . .

```
    comments: MayBe.of(getComments(x.permalink.
    replace("?ref=search_posts",".json")))
```

. . .

Note   We are replacing the permalink value ?ref=search_ posts with .json as search results append the value ?ref=search_posts, which is not the correct format for the getComments API call.

Throughout the full process we haven't come outside our MayBe type. We run our all map functions happily on our MayBe type without worrying about it too much. We solved our problem so elegantly with MayBe, didn't we? There is a slight problem with our MayBe functor that is used this way, though. Let's talk about it in the next section.

Problem of Nested/Many maps

If you count the number of map calls on our MayBe in our mergeViaMayBe function, it is four. You might be wondering why we care about the number of map calls.

Let's try to understand the problem of many *chained* map calls like in mergeViaMayBe. Imagine we want to get a comments array that is returned from mergeViaMayBe. We'll pass our search text functional programming in our mergeViaMayBe function:

```
let answer = mergeViaMayBe("functional programming")
```

after the call answer:

```
MayBe {
  value:
   [ { title: 'ELI5: what is functional programming and how is
   it different from OOP',
       comments: [Object] },
```

```
{ title: 'ELI5 why functional programming seems to be "on
the rise" and how it differs from OOP',
  comments: [Object] } ] }
```

Now let's get the comments object for processing. Because the return value is MayBe, we can map over it:

```
answer.map((result) => {
    //process result.
})
```

The result (which is the value of MayBe) is an array that has title and comments, so let's map over it using our Array's map:

```
answer.map((result) => {
    arrayUtils.map(result,(mergeResults) => {
        //mergeResults
    })
})
```

Each mergeResults is an object, which has title and comments. Remember that comments are also a MayBe. To get comments, therefore, we need to map over our comments:

```
answer.map((result) => {
    arrayUtils.map(result,(mergeResults) => {
        mergeResults.comments.map(comment => {
            //finally got the comment object
        })
    })
})
```

It looks like we have done more work to get the list of comments. Imagine someone is using our mergeViaMayBe API to get the comments list. They will be really irritated to get back the result using nested maps already shown. Can we make our mergeViaMayBe better? Yes we can: Meet monads.

Solving the Problem via join

We saw in previous sections how deep we have to go inside our MayBe to get back our desired results. Writing such APIs is not going to help us, but rather will irritate other developers working on it. To solve these deep-nested issues, let's add join to the MayBe functor.

join Implementation

Let's start implementing the join function. The join function is simple and looks like Listing 9-5.

Listing 9-5. join Function Definition

```
MayBe.prototype.join = function() {
  return this.isNothing() ? MayBe.of(null) : this.value;
}
```

join is very simple and it simply returns the value inside our container (if there are values); if not, it returns MayBe.of(null). join is simple, but it helps us to unwrap the nested MayBes:

```
let joinExample = MayBe.of(MayBe.of(5))

=> MayBe { value: MayBe { value: 5 } }

joinExample.join()
=> MayBe { value: 5 }
```

As shown in this example, it unwraps the nested structure into a single level. Imagine we want to add 4 to our value in joinExample MayBe. Let's give it a try:

```
joinExample.map((outsideMayBe) => {
    return outsideMayBe.map((value) => value + 4)
})
```

196

This code returns the following:

```
MayBe { value: MayBe { value: 9 } }
```

Even though the value is correct, we have mapped twice to get the result. Again the result that we got ends up in a nested structure. Now let's do the same via join:

```
joinExample.join().map((v) => v + 4)

=> MayBe { value: 9 }
```

That code is simply elegant. The call to join returns the inside MayBe, which has the value of 5; once we have that, we are running over it via map and then add the value 4. Now the resulting value is in a *flatten* structure MayBe { value: 9 }.

Now with join in place, let's try to level the nested structure returned by mergeViaMayBe. We'll change the code to Listing 9-6.

Listing 9-6. mergeViaMayBe Using join

```
let mergeViaJoin = (searchText) => {
    let redditMayBe = MayBe.of(searchReddit(searchText))
    let ans = redditMayBe.map((arr) => arr['data'])
              .map((arr) => arr['children'])
              .map((arr) => arrayUtils.map(arr, (x) => {
                  return {
                      title : x['data'].title,
                      permalink : x['data'].permalink
                  }
              }
          ))
```

```
            .map((obj) => arrayUtils.map(obj, (x) => {
                return {
                    title: x.title,
                    comments: MayBe.of(getComments
                    (x.permalink.replace
                    ("?ref=search_posts",".json"))).join()
                }
        }))
        .join()
    return ans;
}
```

As you can see, we have just added two joins in our code. One is on the comments section, where we create a nested MayBe, and another one is right after our all map operation.

Now with mergeViaJoin in place, let's implement the same logic of getting the comments array out of the result. First let's quickly look at the response returned by mergeViaJoin:

```
mergeViaJoin("functional programming")
```

That is going to return the following:

```
[ { title: 'ELI5: what is functional programming and how is it
different from OOP',
    comments: [ [Object], [Object] ] },
  { title: 'ELI5 why functional programming seems to be "on the
  rise" and how it differs from OOP',
    comments: [ [Object], [Object] ] } ]
```

Compare that result with our old `mergeViaMayBe`:

```
MayBe {
  value:
   [ { title: 'ELI5: what is functional programming and how is
   it different from OOP',
      comments: [Object] },
    { title: 'ELI5 why functional programming seems to be "on
    the rise" and how it differs from OOP',
      comments: [Object] } ] }
```

As you can see, `join` has taken out the MayBe's value and sent it back. Now let's see how to use the `comments` array for our processing task. Because the value returned from `mergeViaJoin` is an array, we can map over it using our `Arrays` map:

```
arrayUtils.map(result, mergeResult => {
    //mergeResult
})
```

Now each `mergeResult` variable directly points to the object that has `title` and `comments`. Note that we have called `join` in our MayBe call of `getComments`, so the `comments` object is just a simple array. With that in mind, to get the list of `comments` from the iteration, we just need to call `mergeResult.comments`:

```
arrayUtils.map(result,mergeResult => {
    //mergeResult.comments has the comments array
})
```

This looks promising, as we have gotten the full benefit of our MayBe and also a good data structure to return the results, which are easy for processing.

chain Implementation

Have a look at the code in Listing 9-6. As you can guess, we need to call join always after map. Let's wrap this logic inside a method called chain, as shown in Listing 9-7.

Listing 9-7. chain Function Definition

```
MayBe.prototype.chain = function(f){
  return this.map(f).join()
}
```

Once chain is in place, we can make our merge function logic look like Listing 9-8.

Listing 9-8. mergeViaMayBe Using chain

```
let mergeViaChain = (searchText) => {
    let redditMayBe = MayBe.of(searchReddit(searchText))
    let ans = redditMayBe.map((arr) => arr['data'])
            .map((arr) => arr['children'])
            .map((arr) => arrayUtils.map(arr, (x) => {
                    return {
                        title : x['data'].title,
                        permalink : x['data'].permalink
                    }
                }
            ))
            .chain((obj) => arrayUtils.map(obj, (x) => {
                return {
                    title: x.title,
                    comments: MayBe.of(getComments(x.
                    permalink.replace("?ref=search_posts",
                    ".json"))).join()
                }
```

```
        }))

    return ans;
}
```

The output is going to be exactly the same via chain, too. Play around with this function. In fact, with chain in place, we can move the logic of counting the number of comments to an in-place operation, as shown in Listing 9-9.

Listing 9-9. Making Improvements on mergeViaChain

```
let mergeViaChain = (searchText) => {
    let redditMayBe = MayBe.of(searchReddit(searchText))
    let ans = redditMayBe.map((arr) => arr['data'])
            .map((arr) => arr['children'])
            .map((arr) => arrayUtils.map(arr, (x) => {
                    return {
                        title : x['data'].title,
                        permalink : x['data'].permalink
                    }
                }
            ))
            .chain((obj) => arrayUtils.map(obj, (x) => {
                return {
                    title: x.title,
                    comments: MayBe.of(getComments(x.
                    permalink.replace("?ref=search_posts",".
                    json"))).chain(x => {
                        return x.length
                    })
                }
            }))
    return ans;
}
```

Now calling this code:

```
mergeViaChain("functional programming")
```

will return the following:

```
[ { title: 'ELI5: what is functional programming and how is it
different from OOP',
    comments: 2 },
 { title: 'ELI5 why functional programming seems to be "on the
  rise" and how it differs from OOP',
    comments: 2 } ]
```

The solution looks so elegant, but we still haven't seen a monad, have we?

What Is a Monad?

You might be wondering why we started the chapter with a promise of teaching you about a monad, but still haven't defined what a monad is. We're sorry for not defining the monad, but you have already seen it in action. (What?)

Yes, a monad is a functor that has a chain method; that's it, that's what a monad is. As you have already seen, we have extended our favorite MayBe functor to add a chain (and of course a join function) to make it a monad.

We started with an example of a functor to solve an ongoing problem and ended up solving the problem using a monad without even being aware of using it. That's intentional from our side as we wanted to see the intuition behind monad (the problem it solves with a functor). We could have started with a simple definition of monad, but although that shows *what* a monad is, it won't show *why* a monad should be used.

Note   You might be confused thinking about whether MayBe is a monad or a functor. Don't get confused: MayBe with only of and map is a functor. A functor with `chain` is a monad.

Summary

In this chapter we have seen a new functor type called a monad. We discussed the problem of how repetitive maps will cause nested values, which become difficult to handle later. We introduced a new function called chain, which helps to flatten the MayBe data. We saw that a pointed functor with a chain is called a monad. In this chapter, we were using a third-party library to create Ajax calls. In the next chapter, we will be seeing a new way to think of asynchronous calls.

CHAPTER 10

Pause, Resume, and Async with Generators

We started the book with a simple definition of functions, then we saw how to use functions to do great things using the functional programming technique. We have seen how to handle arrays, objects, and error handling, in pure functional terms. It has been quite a long journey for us, but we still have not talked about yet another important technique that every JavaScript developer should be aware of: asynchronous code.

You have dealt with a great deal of asynchronous codes in your project. You might be wondering whether functional programming can help developers in asynchronous code. The answer is yes and no. The technique that we're going to showcase initially is using ES6 Generators and then using Async/Await, which is a new addition to the ECMAScript 2017/ES8 specification. Both the patterns try to solve the same callback problem in their own way, so pay close attention to the subtle differences. Generators were new specs for functions in ES6. Generators are not really a functional programming technique; however, they are part of a function (functional programming is about function, right?); for that reason we have dedicated a chapter to it in this functional programming book.

© Anto Aravinth, Srikanth Machiraju 2018
A. Aravinth and S. Machiraju, *Beginning Functional JavaScript*,
https://doi.org/10.1007/978-1-4842-4087-8_10

Even if you are a big fan of Promises (which is a technique for solving the callback problem), we still advise you to have a look at this chapter. You are likely to love generators and the way they solve the async code problems.

Note   The chapter examples and library source code are in branch chap10. The repo's URL is https://github.com/antsmartian/functional-es8.git.

Once you check out the code, please check out branch chap10:

git checkout -b chap10 origin/chap10

For running the codes, as before run:

...

npm run playground

...

Async Code and Its Problem

Before we really see what generators are, let's discuss the problem of handling async code in JavaScript in this section. We are going to talk about a callback hell problem. Most of the async code patterns like Generators or Async/Await try to solve the callback hell problem in their own ways. If you already know what it is, feel free to move to the next section. For others, please read on.

Callback Hell

Imagine you have a function like the one shown in Listing 10-1.

Listing 10-1. Synchronous Functions

```
let sync = () => {
        //some operation
        //return data
}

let sync2 = () => {
        //some operation
        //return data
}

let sync3 = () => {
        //some operation
        //return data
}
```

The functions sync, sync1, and sync2 do some operations synchronously and return the results. As a result, one can call these functions like this:

```
result = sync()
result2 = sync2()
result3 = sync3()
```

What if the operation is asynchronous? Let's see it in action in Listing 10-2.

Listing 10-2. Asynchronous Functions

```
let async = (fn) => {
        //some async operation
        //call the callback with async operation
        fn(/*  result data */)
}
```

```
let async2 = (fn) => {
        //some async operation
        //call the callback with async operation
        fn(/* result data */)
}

let async3 = (fn) => {
        //some async operation
        //call the callback with async operation
        fn(/* result data */)
}
```

Synchronous vs. Asynchronous   Synchronous is when the function blocks the caller when it is executing and returns the result once it's available.

Asynchronous is when the function doesn't block the caller when it's executing the function but returns the result once available.

We deal with Asynchronous heavily when we deal with an AJAX request in our project.

Now if someone wants to process these functions at once, how they do it? The only way to do it is shown in Listing 10-3.

Listing 10-3. Async Functions Calling Example

```
async(function(x){
    async2(function(y){
        async3(function(z){

            ...

        });
    });
});
```

Oops! You can see in Listing 10-3 that we are passing many callback functions to our `async` functions. This little piece of code showcases what callback hell is. Callback hell makes the program harder to understand. Handling errors and bubbling the errors out of callback are tricky and always error prone.

Before ES6 arrived, JavaScript developers used Promises to solve this problem. Promises are great, but given the fact that ES6 introduced generators at a language level, we don't need Promises anymore!

Generators 101

As mentioned, generators were part of the ES6 specifications and they are bundled up at language level. We talked about using generators to help with handling async code. Before we get there, though, we are going to talk about the fundamentals of generators. This section focuses on explaining the core concepts behind generators. Once we learn the basics, we can create a generic function using generators to handle async code in our library. Let's begin.

Creating Generators

Let's start our journey by seeing how to create generators in the first place. Generators are nothing but a function that comes up with its own syntax. A simple generator looks like Listing 10-4.

Listing 10-4. First Simple Generator

```
function* gen() {
    return 'first generator';
}
```

209

The function gen in Listing 10-4 is a generator. As you might notice, we have used an asterisk before our function name (in this case gen) to denote that it is a generator function. We have seen how to create a generator; now let's see how to invoke a generator:

```
let generatorResult = gen()
```

What will be the result of generatorResult? Is it going to be a first generator value? Let's print it on the console and inspect it:

```
console.log(generatorResult)
```

The result will be:

```
gen {[[GeneratorStatus]]: "suspended", [[GeneratorReceiver]]:
Window}
```

Caveats of Generators

The preceding examples show how to create a generator, how to create an instance for it, and how it gets values. There are a few important things we need to take care of, though, while we are working with generators.

The first thing is that we cannot call next as many times as we want to get the value from the generator. To make it clearer, let's try to fetch a value from our first generator (refer to Listing 10-4 for the first generator definition):

```
let generatorResult = gen()

//for the first time
generatorResult.next().value
=> 'first generator'

//for the second time
generatorResult.next().value
=> undefined
```

As you can see in this code, calling next for the second time will return an undefined rather than `first generator`. The reason is that generators are like sequences: Once the values of the sequence are consumed, you cannot consume it again. In our case `generatorResult` is a sequence that has value as `first generator`. With our first call to next, we (as the caller of the generator) have consumed the value from the sequence. Because the sequence is empty now, calling it a second time will return you `undefined`.

To consume the sequence again, you need to create another generator instance:

```
let generatorResult = gen()
let generatorResult2 = gen()

//first sequence
generatorResult.next().value
=> 'first generator'

//second sequence
generatorResult2.next().value
=> 'first generator'
```

This code also shows that different instances of generators can be in different states. The key takeaway here is that each generator's state depends on how we are calling the next function on it.

yield Keyword

With generator functions, there is a new keyword that we can use called `yield`. In this section, we are going to see how to use `yield` within a generator function. Let's start with the code in Listing 10-5.

Listing 10-5. Simple Generator Sequence

```
function* generatorSequence() {
    yield 'first';
    yield 'second';
    yield 'third';
}
```

As usual we can create a generator instance for that code:

```
let generatorSequence = generatorSequence();
```

Now if we call next for the first time we get back the value first:

```
generatorSequence.next().value
=> first
```

What happens if we call next again? Do we get first? Or second? Or third? Or an error? Let's find out:

```
generatorSequence.next().value
=> second
```

We got back the value second. Why? yield makes the generator function pause the execution and send back the result to the caller. Therefore when we call generatorSequence for the first time, the function sees the yield with value first, so it puts the function to pause mode and returns the value (and it remembers where it exactly paused, too). The next time we call the generatorSequence (using the same instance variable), the generator function resumes from where it left off. Because it paused at the line:

```
yield 'first';
```

for the first time, when we call it for a second time (using the same instance variable), we get back the value second. What happens when we call it for the third time? Yes, we will get back the value third.

This is better explained by looking at Figure 10-1. This sequence is explained via the code in Listing 10-6.

Listing 10-6. Calling Our Generator Sequence

```
//get generator instance variable
let generatorSequenceResult = generatorSequence();

console.log('First time sequence value',generatorSequenceResult.
next().value)
console.log('Second time sequence value',generatorSequenceResult.
next().value)
console.log('third time sequence value',generatorSequenceResult.
next().value)
```

This prints the following back to the console:

```
First time sequence value first
Second time sequence value second
third time sequence value third
```

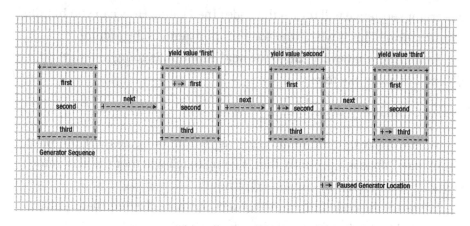

Figure 10-1. *Visual view of generator listed in Listing 10-4*

With that understanding in place, you can see why we call a generator a sequence of values. One more important point to keep in mind is that all generators with `yield` will execute in lazy evaluation order.

Lazy Evaluation   What is lazy evaluation? To put it in simple terms, lazy evaluation means the code won't run until we ask it to run. As you can guess, the example of the `generatorSequence` function shows that generators are lazy evaluated. The values are being executed and returned only when we ask for them. That's so lazy about generators, isn't it?

---

done Property of Generator

Now we have seen how a generator can produce a sequence of values lazily with the `yield` keyword. A generator can also produce n numbers of sequence; as a user of the generator function, how will you know when to stop calling next? Because calling next on your already consumed generator sequence will return the `undefined` value. How can you handle this situation? This is where the done property enters the picture.

Remember that every call to the next function is going to return an object that looks like this:

```
{value: 'value', done: false}
```

We are aware that the `value` is the value from our generator, but what about done? done is a property that is going to tell whether the generator sequence has been fully consumed or not.

We rerun the code from previous sections here (Listing 10-4), just to print the object being returned from the next call.

Listing 10-7. Code for Understanding done Property

```
//get generator instance variable
let generatorSequenceResult = generatorSequence();

console.log('done value for the first time',
generatorSequenceResult.next())
console.log('done value for the second time',
generatorSequenceResult.next())
console.log('done value for the third time',
generatorSequenceResult.next())
```

Running this code will print the following:

```
done value for the first time { value: 'first', done: false }
done value for the second time { value: 'second', done: false }
done value for the third time { value: 'third', done: false }
```

As you can see we have consumed all the values from the generator sequence, so calling next again will return the following object:

```
console.log(generatorSequenceResult.next())
=> { value: undefined, done: true }
```

Now the done property clearly tells us that the generator sequence is already fully consumed. When the done is true, it's time for us to stop calling next on that particular generator instance. This can be better visualized with Figure 10-2.

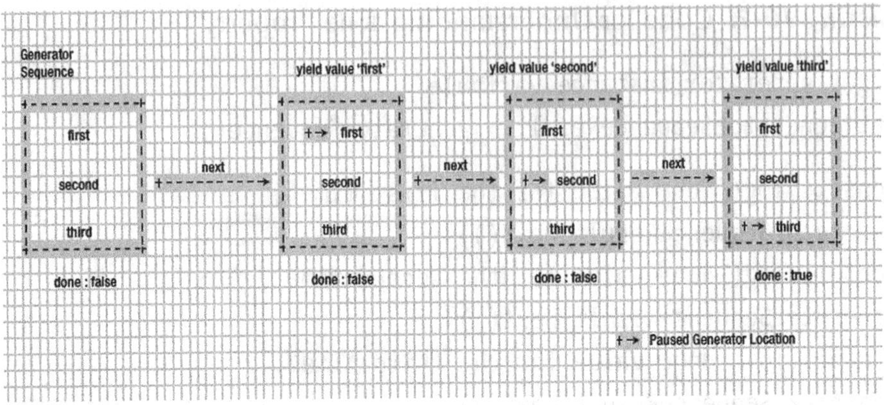

Figure 10-2. View of generators done property for generatorSequence

Because generator became the core part of ES6, we have a for loop that will allow us to iterate a generator (after all it's a sequence):

```
for(let value of generatorSequence())
        console.log("for of value of generatorSequence
        is",value)
```

This is going to print:

```
for of value of generatorSequence is first
for of value of generatorSequence is second
for of value of generatorSequence is third
```

notably for using the generator's done property to iterate through it.

Passing Data to Generators

In this section, let's discuss how we pass data to generators. Passing data to generators might feel confusing at first, but as you will see in this chapter, it makes async programming easy.

Let's take a look at the code in Listing 10-8.

Listing 10-8. Passing Data Generator Example

```
function* sayFullName() {
    var firstName = yield;
    var secondName = yield;
    console.log(firstName + secondName);
}
```

This code now might not be a surprise for you. Let's use this code to explain the concept of passing data to the generator. As always, we create a generator instance first:

```
let fullName = sayFullName()
```

Once the generator instance is created, let's call next on it:

```
fullName.next()
fullName.next('anto')
fullName.next('aravinth')
=> anto aravinth
```

In this code snippet the last call will print anto aravinth to the console. You might be confused with this result, so let's walk through the code slowly. When we call next for the first time:

```
fullName.next()
```

the code will return and pause at the line

```
var firstName = yield;
```

Because here we are not sending any value back via yield, next will return the value undefined. The second call to next is where an interesting thing happens:

```
fullName.next('anto')
```

Here we are passing the value anto to the next call. Now the generator will be resumed from its previous paused state. Remember that the previous paused state is on the line

```
var firstName = yield;
```

Because we have passed the value anto on this call, yield will be replaced by anto and thus firstName holds the value anto. After the value is set to firstName, the execution will be resumed (from the previous paused state) and again sees the yield and stops the execution at

```
var secondName = yield;
```

Now for the third time, if we call next:

```
fullName.next('aravinth')
```

When this line gets executed, our generator will resume from where it paused. The previous paused state is

```
var secondName = yield;
```

As before, the passed value aravinth of our next call will be replaced by yield and aravinth is set to secondName. Then the generator happily resumes the execution and sees this statement:

```
console.log(firstName + secondName);
```

By now, firstName is anto and secondName is aravinth, so the console will print anto aravinth. This full process is illustrated in Figure 10-3.

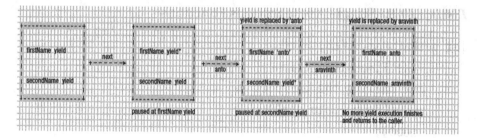

Figure 10-3. *Explaining how data are passed to sayFullName generator*

You might be wondering why we need such an approach. It turns out that using generators by passing data to them makes it very powerful. We use the same technique in the next section to handle async calls.

Using Generators to Handle Async Calls

In this section, we are going to use generators for real-world stuff. We are going to see how passing data to generators makes them very powerful to handle async calls. We are going to have quite a lot of fun in this section.

Generators for Async: A Simple Case

In this section, we are going to see how to use generators for handling async code. Because we are getting started with a different mindset of using generators to solve the async problem, we want to keep things simple, so we will mimic the async calls with setTimeout calls!

Imagine you two functions shown in Listing 10-9 (which are async in nature).

Listing 10-9. Simple Asynchronous Functions

```
let getDataOne = (cb) => {
        setTimeout(function(){
        //calling the callback
        cb('dummy data one')
    }, 1000);
}

let getDataTwo = (cb) => {
        setTimeout(function(){
        //calling the callback
        cb('dummy data two')
    }, 1000);
}
```

Both these functions mimic the async code with setTimeout. Once the desired time has elapsed, setTimeout will call the passed callback cb with value dummy data one and dummy data two, respectively. Let's see how we will be calling these two functions without generators in the first place:

```
getDataOne((data) => console.log("data received",data))
getDataTwo((data) => console.log("data received",data))
```

That code will print the following after 1,000 ms:

```
data received dummy data one
data received dummy data two
```

Now as you notice, we are passing the callbacks to get back the response. We have talked about how bad the callback hell can be in async code. Let's use our generator knowledge to solve the current problem. We now change both the functions getDataOne and getDataTwo to use generator instances rather than callbacks for passing the data.

First let's change the function getDataOne (Listing 10-8) to what is shown in Listing 10-10.

Listing 10-10. Changing getDataOne to Use Generator

```
let generator;
let getDataOne = () => {
        setTimeout(function(){
        //call the generator and
        //pass data via next
        generator.next('dummy data one')
    }, 1000);
}
```

We have changed the callback line from

```
. . .
cb('dummy data one')
. . .
```

to

```
generator.next('dummy data one')
```

That's a simple change. Note that we have also removed the cb, which is not required in this case. We will do the same for getDataTwo (Listing 10-8), too, as shown in Listing 10-11.

Listing 10-11. Changing getDataTwo to Use Generator

```
let getDataTwo = () => {
        setTimeout(function(){
        //call the generator and
        //pass data via next
        generator.next('dummy data two')
    }, 1000);
}
```

Now with that change in place, let's go and test our new code. We'll wrap our call to getDataOne and getDataTwo inside a separate generator function, as shown in Listing 10-12.

Listing 10-12. main Generator Function

```
function* main() {
    let dataOne = yield getDataOne();
    let dataTwo = yield getDataTwo();
    console.log("data one",dataOne)
    console.log("data two",dataTwo)
}
```

Now the main code looks exactly like the sayFullName function from our previous section. Let's create a generator instance for main and trigger the next call and see what happens.

```
generator = main()
generator.next();
```

That will print the following to the console:

```
data one dummy data one
data two dummy data two
```

That is what exactly we wanted. Look at our main code; the code looks like synchronous calls to the functions getDataOne and getDataTwo. However both these calls are asynchronous. Remember that these calls never block and they work in async fashion. Let's distill how this whole process works.

First we are creating a generator instance for main using the generator variable that we declared earlier. Remember that this generator is used by both getDataOne and getDataTwo to push the data to its call, which we will see soon. After creating the instance, we are firing the whole process with the line

```
generator.next()
```

This calls the main function. The main function is put into execution and we see the first line with yield:

```
. . .
let dataOne = yield getDataOne();
. . .
```

Now the generator will be put into pause mode as it has seen a yield statement. Before it's been put into pause mode, though, it calls the function getDataOne.

Note An important point here is that even though the yield makes the statement pause, it won't make the caller wait (i.e., caller is not blocked). To make the point more concrete, see the following code.

```
generator.next() //even though the generator pause
for Async codes
console.log("will be printed")
=> will be printed
=> Generator data result is printed
```

This code shows that even though our generator.next causes the generator function to wait on the next call, the caller (the one who is calling the generator) won't be blocked! As you can see, console.log will be printed (showcasing generator.next isn't blocked), and then we get the data from the generator once the async operation is done.

Now interestingly the getDataOne function has the following line in its body:

```
. . .
    generator.next('dummy data one')
. . .
```

As we discussed earlier, calling next by passing a parameter will resume the paused yield, and that's exactly what happens here in this case. Remember that this piece of line is inside setTimeout, so it will get executed only when 1,000 ms have elapsed. Until then, the code will be paused at the line

```
let dataOne = yield getDataOne();
```

One more important point to note here is that while this line is paused, the timeout will be running down from 1,000 to 0. Once it reaches 0, it is going to execute the line

```
. . .
    generator.next('dummy data one')
. . .
```

That is going to send back dummy data one to our yield statement, so the dataOne variable becomes dummy data one:

```
//after 1,000 ms dataOne becomes
//'dummy data one'
let dataOne = yield getDataOne();
=> dataOne = 'dummy data one'
```

That's a lot of interesting stuff happening. Once dataOne is set to the dummy data one value, the execution will continue to the next line:

```
. . .
let dataTwo = yield getDataTwo();
. . .
```

This line is going to run the same way as the line before! So after the execution of this line, we have dataOne and dataTwo:

```
dataOne = dummy data one
dataTwo = dummy data two
```

That is what is getting printed to the console at the final statements of the main function:

```
. . .
    console.log("data one",dataOne)
    console.log("data two",dataTwo)
. . .
```

The full process is shown in Figure 10-4.

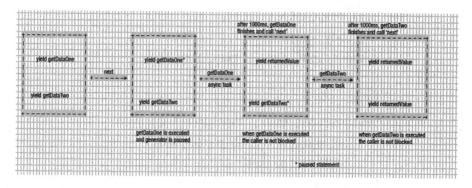

Figure 10-4. *Image explaining how* main *generator works internally*

Now you have made an asynchronous call look like a synchronous call, but it works in an asynchronous way.

Generators for Async: A Real-World Case

In the previous section, we saw how to handle asynchronous code using generators effectively. To mimic the async workflow we used setTimeout. In this section, we are going to use a function to fire a real AJAX call to Reddit APIs to showcase the power of generators in the real world.

To make an async call, let's create a function called httpGetAsync, shown in Listing 10-13.

Listing 10-13. httpGetAsync Function Definition

```
let https = require('https');
function httpGetAsync(url,callback) {

    return https.get(url,
        function(response) {
            var body = ";
            response.on('data', function(d) {
                body += d;
            });
            response.on('end', function() {
                let parsed = JSON.parse(body)
                callback(parsed)
            })
        }
    );

}
```

This is a simple function that uses an https module from a node to fire an AJAX call to get the response back.

Note   Here we are not going to see in detail how `httpGetAsync` function works. The problem we are trying to solve is how to convert functions like `httpGetAsync`, which works the async way but expects a callback to get the response from AJAX calls.

Let's check `httpGetAsync` by passing a Reddit URL:

```
httpGetAsync('https://www.reddit.com/r/pics/.json',(data)=> {
        console.log(data)
})
```

It works by printing the data to the console. The URL `https://www.reddit.com/r/pics/.json` prints the list of JSON about the Picture Reddit page. The returned JSON has a `data` key with a structure that looks like the following:

```
{ modhash: ",
  children:
   [ { kind: 't3', data: [Object] },
     { kind: 't3', data: [Object] },
     { kind: 't3', data: [Object] },
     . . .
     { kind: 't3', data: [Object] } ],
  after: 't3_5bzyli',
  before: null }
```

Imagine we want to get the URL of the first `children` of the array; we need to navigate to `data.children[0].data.url`. This will give us a URL like `https://www.reddit.com/r/pics/comments/5bqai9/introducing_new_rpics_title_guidelines/`. Because we need to get the JSON format of the given URL, we need to append `.json` to the URL, so that it becomes `https://www.reddit.com/r/pics/comments/5bqai9/introducing_new_rpics_title_guidelines/.json`.

Now let's see that in action:

```
httpGetAsync('https://www.reddit.com/r/pics/.json',(picJson)=>
{
    httpGetAsync(picJson.data.children[0].data.url+".
    json",(firstPicRedditData) => {
        console.log(firstPicRedditData)
    })
})
```

This code will print the data as required. We are least worried about the data being printed, but we are worried about our code structure. As we saw at the beginning of this chapter, code that looks like this suffers from callback hell. Here there are two levels of callbacks, which might not be a real problem, but what if it goes to four or five nested levels? Can you read such codes easily? Definitely not. Now let's find out how to solve the problem via generator.

Let's wrap httpGetAsync inside a separate method called request, shown in Listing 10-14.

Listing 10-14. request Function

```
function request(url) {
    httpGetAsync( url, function(response){
        generator.next( response );
    } );
}
```

We have removed the callback with the generator's next call, very similar to our previous section. Now let's wrap our requirement inside a generator function; again we call it main, as shown in Listing 10-15.

Listing 10-15. main Generator Function

```
function *main() {
    let picturesJson = yield request( "https://www.reddit.
    com/r/pics/.json" );
    let firstPictureData = yield request(picturesJson.data.
    children[0].data.url+".json")
    console.log(firstPictureData)
}
```

This main function looks very similar to the main function we defined in Listing 10-11 (the only change is the method call details). In the code we are yielding on two calls to request. As we saw in the setTimeout example, calling yield on request will make it pause until request calls the generator next by sending the AJAX response back. The first yield will get the JSON of pictures, and the second yield gets the first picture data by calling request, respectively. Now we have made the code look like synchronous code, but in reality, it works in an asynchronous fashion.

We have also escaped from callback hell using generators. Now the code looks clean and clearly tells what it's doing. That's so much more powerful for us!

Try running it:

```
generator = main()
generator.next()
```

It's going to print the data as required. We have clearly seen how to use generators to convert any function that expects a callback mechanism into a generator-based one. In turn, we get back clean code for handling an asynchronous operation.

Async Functions in ECMAScript 2017

So far, we have seen multiple ways to run functions asynchronously. Primitively the only way to perform background jobs was by using a callback, but we just learned how they result in callback hell. Generators or sequences provide one way of solving the callback hell problem using the `yield` operator and generator functions. As part of the ECMA8 script, two new operators are introduced, called `async` and `await`. These two new operators solve the callback hell problem by introducing a modern design pattern for authoring asynchronous code using `Promise`.

Promise

If you are already aware of Promises you can skip this section. A Promise in JavaScript world is piece of work that is expected to complete (or fail) at some point in the future. For example, parents might Promise to give their child an XBOX if they get an A+ on an upcoming test, as represented by the following code.

```
let grade = "A+";
let examResults = new Promise(
    function (resolve, reject) {
        if (grade == "A+")
            resolve("You will get an XBOX");
        else
            reject("Better luck next time");
    }
);
```

Now, the `Promise` examResults when consumed can be in any of three states: pending, resolved, or rejected. The following code shows a sample consumption of the preceding Promise.

```
let conductExams = () => {
    examResults
    .then(x => console.log(x)) // captures resolve and logs
    "You will get an XBOX"
    .catch(x => console.error(x)); // captures rejection and
    logs "Better luck next time"
};

conductExams();
```

Now if you have successfully relearned the philosophy of Promise, we can understand what async and await do.

Await

An await is a keyword that can be prepended to a function if the function returns a Promise object, thus making it run in the background. Usually a function or another Promise is used to consume a Promise, and await simplifies the code by allowing the Promise to resolve in the background. In other words, the await keyword waits for the Promise to resolve or fail. Once the Promise is resolved, the data returned by the Promise—either resolved or rejected—can be consumed, but meanwhile the main flow of the application is unblocked to perform any other important tasks. The rest of the execution unfolds when the Promise completes.

Async

A function that uses await should be marked as async.

Let us understand the usage of async and await using the following example.

```
function fetchTextByPromise() {
    return new Promise(resolve => {
        setTimeout(() => {
```

```
        resolve("es8");
    }, 2000);
});
}
```

Before ES8 can consume this Promise, you might have to wrap it in a function as shown in the preceding example or use another Promise as shown here.

```
function sayHello() {
    return new Promise((resolve, reject) => fetchTextByPromise()
  .then(x => console.log(x))
        .catch(x => console.error(x)));
}
```

Now, here is a much simpler and cleaner version using async and await.

```
async function sayHello() {
    const externalFetchedText = await fetchTextByPromise();
    console.log(`Response from SayHello: Hello,
${externalFetchedText}`);
}
```

We can also write using arrow syntax as shown here.

```
let sayHello = async () => {
    const externalFetchedText = await fetchTextByPromise();
    console.log(`Response from SayHello: Hello,
    ${externalFetchedText}`); // Hello, es8
}
```

You can consume this method by simply calling

```
sayHello()
```

Chaining Callbacks

The beauty of `async` and `await` is harder to understand until we see some sample uses of remote API calls. What follows is an example where we call a remote API that returns a JSON array. We silently wait for the array to arrive and process the first object and make another remote API call. The important thing to learn here is that while all this is happening, the main thread can work on something else because the remote API calls might take some time; hence the network call and corresponding processing is happening in the background.

Here is the function that invokes a remote URL and returns a Promise.

```
// returns a Promise
const getAsync = (url) => {
    return fetch(url)
        .then(x => x)
        .catch(x =>
            console.log("Error in getAsync:" + x)
        );
}
```

The next function consumes getAsync.

```
// 'async' can only be used in functions where 'await' is used
async function getAsyncCaller() {
    try {
        // https://jsonplaceholder.typicode.com/users is a
        sample API which returns a JSON Array of dummy users
        const response = await getAsync("https://
        jsonplaceholder.typicode.com/users"); // pause until
        Promise completes
        const result = await response.json(); //removing .json
        here demonstrates the error handling in Promises
```

233

```
        console.log("GetAsync fetched " + result.length + "
        results");
        return result;
    } catch (error) {
        await Promise.reject("Error in getAsyncCaller:" +
        error.message);
    }
}
```

The following code is used to invoke the flow.

```
getAsyncCaller()
    .then(async (x) => {
        console.log("Call to GetAsync function completed");
        const website = await getAsync("http://" + x[0].
        website);
        console.log("The website (http://" + x[0].website + ")
        content length is " + website.toString().length + "
        bytes");
    })
    .catch(x => console.log("Error: " + x)); // Promise.Reject
    is caught here, the error message can be used to perform
    custom error handling
```

Here is the output for the preceding invocation:

```
This message is displayed while waiting for async operation to
complete, you can do any compute here...
GetAsync fetched 10 results
Call to GetAsync function completed
The website (http://hildegard.org) content length is 17 bytes
```

As you can see, the code execution continues and prints the following console statement, which is the last statement in the program, while the remote API call is happening in the background. Any code following this also gets executed.

```
console.log("This message is displayed while waiting for async
operation to complete, you can do any compute here...");
```

The following result is available when the first await completes; that is, the first API call is completed, and the results are enumerated.

```
This message is displayed while waiting for async operation to
complete, you can do any compute here...
GetAsync fetched 10 results
Call to GetAsync function completed
```

At this point the control returns to the caller, getAsyncCaller in this case, and the call is again awaited by the async call, which makes another remote call using the website property. Once the final API call is completed, the data are returned to the website object and the following block is executed:

```
const website = await getAsync("http://" + x[0].
website);
console.log("The website (http://" + x[0].website + ")
content length is " + website.toString().length + "
bytes");
```

You can observe that we have made dependent remote API calls asynchronously, yet the code appears flat and readable, so the call hierarchy can grow to any extent without involving any callback hierarchies.

Error Handling in Async Calls

As explained earlier, Promises can be rejected as well (say the Remote API is not available or the JSON format is incorrect). In such cases the consumer's catch block is invoked, which can be used to perform any custom exception handling, as shown here.

```
await Promise.reject("Error in getAsyncCaller:" +
error.message);
```

The error can be bubbled to the caller's catch block as well, as shown next. To simulate an error, remove the .json function getAsyncCaller (read the comments for more details). Also, observe the async usage in the then handler here. Because the dependent remote call uses await the arrow function can be tagged as async.

```
getAsyncCaller()
    .then(async (x) => {
        console.log("Call to GetAsync function completed");
        const website = await getAsync("http://" + x[0].
        website);
        console.log("The website (http://" + x[0].website + ")
        content length is " + website.toString().length + "
        bytes");
    })
    .catch(x => console.log("Error: " + x)); // Promise.Reject
    is caught here, the error message can be used to perform
    custom error handling
```

The new asynchronous pattern is more readable, includes less code, is linear, and is better than the previous ones, making it an instinctive replacement for the previous patterns. Figure 10-5 shows the browser support at the time of writing. For latest information, you can check the browser support from https://caniuse.com/#feat=async-functions.

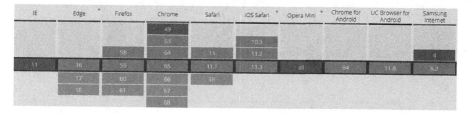

Figure 10-5. *Asynchronous browser support. Source:* `https://caniuse.com/#feat=async-functions`

Async Functions Transpiled to Generators

Async and await have an awfully close relationship with generators. In fact, Babel transpiles async and await to generators in the background, which is quite evident if you look at the transpiled code.

```
let sayHello = async () => {
    const externalFetchedText = await new Promise(resolve => {
        setTimeout(() => {
            resolve("es8");
        }, 2000)});
    console.log(`Response from SayHello: Hello,
    ${externalFetchedText}`);
}
```

For example, the preceding async function will be transpiled to the following code, and you can use any online Babel transpiler like `https://babeljs.io` to watch the transformation. Detailed explanation of the transpiled code is beyond the scope of this book but you might notice that the keyword async is converted into a wrapper function called _asyncToGenerator (line 3). _asyncToGenerator is a routine that Babel adds. This function will be pulled into the transpiled code for any piece of code that uses the async keyword. The crux of our preceding code is converted into a switch case statement (lines 41–59) where each line of code is transpiled into a case as shown here.

```
 1  "use strict";
 2
 3  ⊞ function _asyncToGenerator(fn) { ⋯
32  }
33
34  var sayHello = (function() {
35    var _ref = _asyncToGenerator(
36      regeneratorRuntime.mark(function _callee() {
37        var externalFetchedText;
38        return regeneratorRuntime.wrap(
39          function _callee$(_context) {
40            while (1) {
41              switch ((_context.prev = _context.next)) {
42 ⊞              case 0: ⋯
50 ⊞              case 2: ⋯
56              case 4:
57              case "end":
58                return _context.stop();
59            }
60          }
61        },
62        _callee,
63        this
64      );
65    })
66  );
67
68  return function sayHello() {
69    return _ref.apply(this, arguments);
70  };
71  })();
72
```

Nevertheless `async/await` and generators are the two most prominent ways of authoring linear-looking asynchronous functions in JavaScript. The decision on which one to use is purely a matter of choice. The `async/await` pattern makes async code look like sync and therefore increases readability, whereas generators provide finer control over the state changes within the generator and two-way communication between the caller and the callee.

Summary

The world is full of AJAX calls. There was a time when handling AJAX calls we needed to pass a callback to process the result. Callbacks have their own limitations. Too many callbacks create callback hell problems, for example. We have seen in this chapter a type in JavaScript called generator. Generators are functions that can be paused and resumed using the next method. The next method is available on all generator instances. We have seen how to pass data to generator instances using the next method. The technique of sending data to generators helps us to solve the asynchronous code problem. We have seen how to use generators to make asynchronous code look synchronous, which is an immensely powerful technique for any JavaScript developer. Generators are one way of solving the callback hell problem, but ES8 offers another intuitive way to solve the same problem using `async` and `await`. The new asynchronous pattern is transpiled into generators in the background by compilers like Babel and uses the `Promise` object. Async/await can be used to write linear asynchronous functions in a simple, elegant manner. Await (an equivalent of `yield` in generators) can be used with any function that returns a `Promise` object and a function should be tagged async if it uses `await` anywhere within the body. The new patterns also make error handling easy, as the exceptions raised by both synchronous and asynchronous code can be handled in an equivalent manner.

CHAPTER 11

Building a React-Like Library

So far, we have learned to write functional JavaScript code and to appreciate the modularity, reusability, and simplicity it brings to your applications. We have seen concepts like composition, filters, map, reduce, and other features such as async, await, and pipes. Nonetheless, we have not combined these features together to build a reusable library. That is something we are going to learn in this chapter. In this chapter we build a complete library that will be helpful in building applications, just like React or HyperApp (https://hyperapp.js.org). This chapter is dedicated towards building applications instead of just functions. We will build two HTML applications using functional JavaScript programming concepts we have learned so far. We will learn how to build an application with central storage, render a user interface (UI) using declarative syntax, and wire up events using our custom library. We are going to build a tiny JavaScript library that will be capable of rendering HTML applications with behavior. In the next chapter we will learn to write unit tests for the library we build in this chapter.

Before we start building a library, we need to understand a very important concept in JavaScript called immutability.

© Anto Aravinth, Srikanth Machiraju 2018
A. Aravinth and S. Machiraju, *Beginning Functional JavaScript*,
https://doi.org/10.1007/978-1-4842-4087-8_11

> **Note**   The chapter examples and library source code are in branch chap11. The repo's URL is https://github.com/antsmartian/functional-es8.git.

Once you check out the code, please check out branch chap11:

```
git checkout -b chap11 origin/chap11
```

Open the command prompt as administrator, navigate to the folder that contains package.json, and run

```
npm install
```

to download the packages required for the code to run.

Immutability

JavaScript functions act on data, which are typically stored in variables like strings, arrays, or objects. The state of data is usually defined as the value of the variable at any given point in time. For example:

```
let x = 5; // the state of x is 5 here
let y = x; // the state of y is same as that of x

y = x * 2; // we are altering the state of y

console.log('x = ' + x); // prints: x=5; x is intact,
pretty simple
console.log('y = ' + y); // prints: y=10
```

Now consider string data type:

```
let x = 'Hello'; // the state of x is Hello here
let y = x; // the state of y is same as x
```

```
x = x + ' World'; // altering the state of x

console.log('x = ' + x);  // prints: x = Hello World
console.log('y = ' + y);  // prints: y = y = Hello ; Value of y
is intact
```

So, to conclude JavaScript numbers and strings are immutable. The state of these variable types cannot be altered after it is created. That is not the case with objects and arrays, however. Consider this example:

```
let x = { foo : 'Hello' };
let y = x; // the state of y should be the same as x

x.foo +=  ' World'; // altering the state of x

console.log('x = ' + x.foo); // prints: x = Hello World
console.log('y = ' + y.foo); // prints: y = Hello World; y is
also impacted
```

JavaScript objects and arrays are mutable, and the state of a mutable object can be modified after creation.

Note   This also implies that equality is not a reliable operator for mutable objects because changing a value in one place will update all references.

Here is an example for arrays.

```
let x = [ 'Red', 'Blue'];
let y = x;

x.push('Green');

console.log('x = ' + x); // prints [ 'Red', 'Blue', 'Green' ]
console.log('y = ' + y); // prints [ 'Red', 'Blue', 'Green' ]
```

If you would like to enforce immutability onto JavaScript objects, it is possible by using Object.freeze. Freeze makes the object read-only. For example, consider this code:

```
let x = { foo : 'Hello' };
let y = x;

Object.freeze(x);

// y.foo +=  ' World';
// uncommenting the above line will throw an error, both x and
y are made read-only.

console.log('x = ' + x.foo);
console.log('y = ' + y.foo);
```

To summarize, Table 11-1 differentiates the mutable and immutable types in JavaScript.

Table 11-1. Data Types in JavaScript

Immutable Types	Mutable Types
Numbers, strings	Objects, arrays

Immutability is a very important concept for building modular JavaScript libraries that can be reused across projects. An application's life cycle is driven by its state, and JavaScript applications store state mostly in mutable objects. To predict the state of an application at any given point in time is critical.

In the next section we build a library that can be used as a predictable state container. In this library we use immutability and various functional programming concepts we have learned earlier.

Building a Simple Redux Library

Redux is a library that is inspired by popular single application architectues like Flux, CQRS, and Event Sourcing. Redux helps you centralize the application state and helps you build a predictable state pattern. Before understanding what Redux is, let us try to understand how state is handled in few popular JavaScript frameworks. Let us take Angular as an example. Angular applications rely on the Document Object Model (DOM) to store state, the data is bound to UI components called views (or DOM), the views represent the model, and in turn model changes can update the views. When the application scales horizontally over time as you add new features, it becomes highly challenging to predict the cascading effect of state change. At any given point in time the state can be changed by any component in the application or another model, which makes it extremely unpredictable to determine when and what has caused the application state to change. React, on the other hand, works using virtualized DOM. Given any state, a React application creates a virtual DOM and can then render the virtual DOM.

Redux is a framework-agnostic state library. It can be used with Angular, React, or any other application. Redux is built to address the common problems with application state and how they are influenced by models and views. Redux is inspired by Flux, an application architecture introduced by Facebook. Redux uses a unidirectional flow of data. The following are the design principles of Redux.

- *Single source of truth:* The application has a central state.

- *State is read-only:* Special events called actions describe the state change.

- *Changes are made by pure functions:* Actions are consumed by reducers, and reducers are pure functions that can be invoked when user action is identified. Only one change takes place at a time.

The key feature of Redux is that there is a single source of truth (state). The state is inherently read-only, so the only way to change the state is to emit an action describing what happened. The action is consumed by the reducer and a new state is created, which in turn triggers a DOM update. The actions can be stored and replayed, which allows us to do things like time travel debugging. If you're still confused, do not worry; read on as the pattern is unveiled and becomes simpler when we start implementing it using what we have learned so far.

Figure 11-1 shows how Redux implements predictable state container.

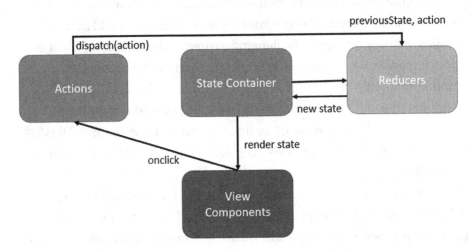

Figure 11-1. *Redux implementation of a state container*

The key ingredients of Redux are reducers, actions, and state. With this context, let's start building our own Redux library.

Note   The Redux library we build here is not production ready; rather, the Redux example is used to demonstrate the power of functional JavaScript programming.

Create a new folder for the Redux library and create a new file called redux.js that will host our library. Copy and paste the code from the following sections into this file. You can use any JavaScript editor of your choice; for example, VS Code. The first and most important part of our Redux library is state. Let's declare a simple state with one property called counter.

```
let initialState = {counter: 0};
```

The next key ingredient is reducer, the only function that can alter the state. A reducer takes two inputs: the current state and an action that acts on the current state and creates a new state. The following function acts as reducer in our library:

```
function reducer(state, action) {
  if (action.type === 'INCREMENT') {
    state = Object.assign({}, state, {counter: state.counter + 1})
  }
  return state;
}
```

In Chapter 4 we discussed the usage of Object.assign for creating new state by merging old states. This method is very helpful when you want to get around the mutability. The reducer function is responsible for creating a new state without altering the current state. You can see how we have used object.assign to achive this: object.assign is used to create a new state by merging two states into one, without affecting the state object.

The action is dispatched by a user interaction; in our example it is a simple button click as shown here.

```
document.getElementById('button').addEventListener('click',
function() {
    incrementCounter();
  });
```

247

When the user clicks a button with Id button the incrementCounter is invoked. Here is the code for incrementCounter:

```
function incrementCounter() {
  store.dispatch({
    type: 'INCREMENT'
  });
}
```

What is store? store is the main function that encapsulates behaviors that cause the state to change, invokes listeners for state change like UI, and registers listeners for the actions. A default listener in our case is the view renderer. The following function elaborates how a store looks.

```
function createStore(reducer,preloadedState){
  let currentReducer = reducer;
    let currentState = preloadedState;
    let currentListeners = [];
    let nextListeners = currentListeners;

    function getState() {
      return currentState;
    }

    function dispatch(action) {
        currentState = currentReducer(currentState, action);

        const listeners = currentListeners = nextListeners;
      for (let i = 0; i < listeners.length; i++) {
        const listener = listeners[i];
        listener();
      }

      return action;
    }
```

```
function subscribe(listener) {
  nextListeners.push(listener);
}

return {
  getState,
  dispatch,
  subscribe
};
}
```

The following code is our one and only listener that renders the UI when there is a change in state.

```
function render(state) {
  document.getElementById('counter').textContent = state.
counter;
}
```

The following code shows how the listener is subscribed using the subscribe method.

```
store.subscribe(function() {
  render(store.getState());
});
```

This code is used to bootstrap the application:

```
let store = createStore(reducer, initialState);
function loadRedux(){
    // Render the initial state
    render(store.getState());
}
```

It is time to plug our Redux library into an application, create a new file called index.html under the same folder, and paste in the following code.

```
<html>
<head>
        <h1>Chapter 11 - Redux Sample</h1>
</head>
<body>
        <h1 id="counter">-</h1>
        <button id="button">Increase</button>
        <script src="./redux.js"></script>
</body>
</html>
```

The function loadRedux is invoked on page load. Let us understand the life cycle of our application.

1. *On load:* Redux store object is created and listener is registered using store.subscribe. The onclick event is also registered to call the reducer.

2. *On click:* The dispatcher is invoked, which creates a new state and invokes the listener.

3. *On render:* The listener (render function) gets the updated state and renders the new view.

This cycle continues until the application is unloaded or destroyed. You can either open index.html in a new file or update package.json with the following code (to see the details of the full package.json, check out the branch mentioned at the beginning of the chapter).

```
"scripts": {
    "playground" : "babel-node functional-playground/play.js
    --presets es2015-node5",
    "start" : "open functional-playground/index.html"
  }
```

To run the application you can run this command, which opens `index.html` in the browser:

```
npm run start
```

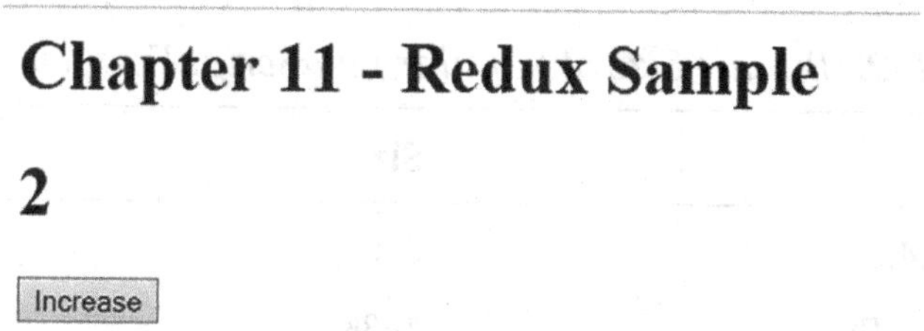

Chapter 11 - Redux Sample

2

[Increase]

Figure 11-2. *Example using our redux library*

Notice that each action performed on the UI is stored in the Redux store, which adds tremendous value to our project. If you want to know the reason for the current state of the application, just traverse through all actions performed on the initial state and replay them; this feature is also called time traveling. This pattern also helps you undo or redo a state change at any point in time. For example, you might want the user to make some changes in the UI but only commit them based on certain validation. If the validation fails you can easily undo the state. Redux can also be used with non-UI applications; remember, it is a state container with time travel capabilities. If you want to know more about Redux, visit `https://redux.js.org/`.

Building a Framework Like HyperApp

Frameworks help reduce development time by allowing us to build on something that already exists and to develop applications within less time. The most common assumption with frameworks is that all the common concerns like caching, garbage collection, state management, and DOM rendering (applicable to UI frameworks only) are addressed. It would be like reinventing the wheel if you start to build an application without

251

any of these frameworks. However, most of the frameworks available in the market to build a single-page UI application suffer from a common problem: bundle size. Table 11-2 provides the gzipped bundle size of most popular modern JavaScript frameworks.

Table 11-2. *Bundle Size of Popular JavaScript Frameworks*

Name	Size
Angular 1.4.5	51K
Angular 2 + Rx	143K
React 16.2.0 + React DOM	31.8K
Ember 2.2.0	111K

Source: https://gist.github.com/Restuta/cda69e50a853aa64912d

HyperApp, on the other hand, Promises to be the thinnest JavaScript framework available to build UI applications. The gzipped version of HyperApp is 1 KB. Why are we talking about a library that is already built? The idea behind this section is not to introduce or to build applications with HyperApp. HyperApp builds on top of functional programming concepts like immutability, closures, higher order functions, and so on. That's the primary reason we are learning to build a Hyper-App-like library.

Because HyperApp needs JSX (JavaScript Extension) syntax to be parsed, and so on, we will learn what Virtual Dom and JSX are in the upcoming sections.

Virtual DOM

DOM is a universally accepted language to represent documents like HTML. Each node in an HTML DOM represents an element in an HTML document. For example:

```
<div>
<h1>Hello, Alice </h1>
<h2>Logged in Date: 16th June 2018</h2>
</div>
```

JavaScript frameworks used to build UI applications intend to build and interact with DOM in a most efficient way. Angular, for example, uses a component-based approach. An application built using Angular contains multiple components, each storing part of the applicaion state locally at the component level. The state is mutable, and every state change rerenders the view, and any user interaction can update the state. For example, the preceding HTML DOM can be written in Angular as shown here:

```
<div>
<h1>Hello, {{username}} </h1>  → Component 1
<h2>Logged in Date: {{dateTime}}</h2>  → Component 2
</div>
```

The variables username and dateTime are stored on the component. Unfortunately, DOM manipulations are costly. Although this is a very popular model, it has various caveats, and here are a few.

1. *The state is not central:* The application's state is locally stored in components and passed across components, resulting in uncertainty of overall state and its transition at any given point in time.

2. *Direct DOM manipulation:* Every state change triggers a DOM update, so in a large application with 50 or more controls on a page the impact on the performance is pretty evident.

To solve these problems we would need a JavaScript framework that can centralize storage and reduce DOM manipulations. In the previous section we learned about Redux, which can be used to build a central predictable state container. The DOM manipulations can be reduced by using Virtual DOM.

Virtual DOM is an in-memory representation of DOM using JSON. The DOM operations are done on the in-memory representation before they are applied to the actual DOM. Based on the framework, the representation of DOM varies. The HyperApp library we discussed earlier uses Virtual DOM to detect the changes during state change and only re-creates the delta DOM, which leads to an increase in the overall efficiency of the application. The following is a sample representation of DOM used by HyperApp.

```
{
  name: "div",
  props: {
    id: "app"
  },
  children: [{
    name: "h1",
    props: null,
    children: ["Hello, Alice"]
  }]
}
```

Virtual DOM is heavily used in the React framework, which uses JSX to represent DOM.

JSX

JSX is a syntax extension of JavaScript that can be used to represent DOM. Here is an example of JSX:

```
const username = "Alice"
const h1 = <h1>Hello, {username}</h1>; //HTML DOM embedded in JS
```

React heavily uses JSX but it can live without it, too. You can put any valid JavaScript expression into the JSX expression like calling a function as shown next.

```
const username = "aliCe";
const h1 = <h1>Hello, {toTitleCase(username)}</h1>;

let toTitleCase = (str) => {
    // logic to convert string to title case here
}
```

We will not be delving into JSX concepts; the idea behind introducing JSX and Virtual DOM is to familiarize you with the concepts. To learn more about JSX please visit https://reactjs.org/docs/introducing-jsx.html.

JS Fiddle

In all the previous chapters we have executed code from our development machines. In this section we introduce an online code editor and compiler called JS Fiddle (https://jsfiddle.net). JS Fiddle can be used to code, debug, and collaborate over HTML, JavaScript, and Cascading Style Sheets (CSS)-based applications. JS Fiddle contains ready-to-use templates and it supports multiple languages, frameworks, and extensions. JS Fiddle is the best tool to use if you're planning to do quick and dirty POCs (Proof of Concepts) or learn something interesting as in this book. It allows you to save work online and work from anywhere, relieving us from the need to set up an appropriate development environment for any new combination of language, compiler, and library.

Figure 11-3. *The image below shows JSFiddle editor*

Let us start building our library by creating a new JS Fiddle. Click
Save on the top ribbon anytime you wish you save the code. As shown in
Figure 11-4, in the Language drop-down list box, select Babel + JSX. In the
Frameworks & Extensions drop-down list box, select No-Library (Pure JS).
Selecting the right combination of language and framework is very
important for the library to compile.

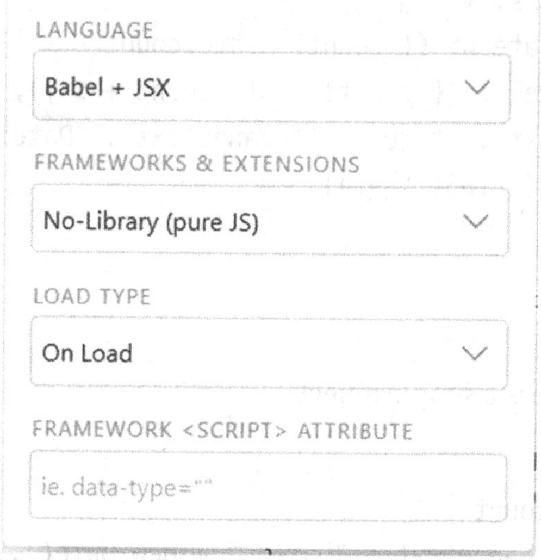

LANGUAGE

Babel + JSX   ∨

FRAMEWORKS & EXTENSIONS

No-Library (pure JS)   ∨

LOAD TYPE

On Load   ∨

FRAMEWORK <SCRIPT> ATTRIBUTE

ie. data-type=""

Figure 11-4. *The below image shows Framework and Exteions*
selection for this code sample

Our library consists of three main components: state, view, and actions
(like HyperApp). The following function acts as a bootstrap for our library.
Paste this code into the JavaScript + No-Library (Pure JS) code section.

```
function main() {
    app({ view: (state, actions) =>
      <div>
          <button onclick={actions.up}>Increase</button>
        <button onclick={actions.down}>Decrease</button>
        <button onclick={actions.changeText}>Change Text</button>
        <p>{state.count}</p>
        <p>{state.changeText}</p>
        </div>,
      state : {
          count : 5,
        changeText : "Date: " + new Date().toString()
        },
```

```
     actions: {
   down: state => ({ count: state.count - 1 }),
   up: state => ({ count: state.count + 1 }),
   changeText : state => ({changeText : "Date: " +
   new Date().toString()})
  }
 })
}
```

The state here is a simple object.

```
state : {
                count : 5,
                changeText : "Date: " + new Date().toString()
}
```

The actions do not change the state directly, but return a new state every time the action is called. The functions down, up, and changeText act on the state object passed as a parameter and return a new state object.

```
actions: {
       down: state => ({ count: state.count - 1 }),
       up: state => ({ count: state.count + 1 }),
       changeText : state => ({changeText : "Date: " + new
Date().toString()})
}
```

The view uses JSX syntax representing a Virtual DOM. The DOM elements are bound to the state object and the events are registered to the actions.

```
<div>
            <button onclick={actions.up}>Increase</button>
            <button onclick={actions.down}>Decrease</button>
```

```
          <button onclick={actions.changeText}>Change Text
          </button>
          <p>{state.count}</p>
          <p>{state.changeText}</p>
</div>
```

The app function shown here is the crux of our library, which accepts state, view, and actions as a single JavaScript object and renders the actual DOM. Copy the following code into the JavaScript + No-Library (Pure JS) section.

```
function app(props){
let appView = props.view;
let appState = props.state;
let appActions = createActions({}, props.actions)
let firstRender = false;
let node = h("p",{},"")
}
```

The function h is inspired from HyperApp, which creates a JavaScript object representation of DOM. This function is basically responsible for creating an in-memory representation of the DOM that is rendered when the state changes. The following function, when called during pageLoad, creates an empty <p></p> node. Copy this code into the JavaScript + No-Library (Pure JS) section.

```
//transformer code
function h(tag, props) {
  let node
  let children = []

  for (i = arguments.length; i-- > 2; ) {
    stack.push(arguments[i])
  }
```

```
while (stack.length) {
  if (Array.isArray((node = stack.pop())))) {
    for (i = node.length; i--; ) {
      stack.push(node[i])
    }
  } else if (node != null && node !== true && node !== false)
{

    children.push(typeof node === "number" ?
    (node = node + "") : node)
  }
}

return typeof tag === "string"
  ? {
      tag: tag,
      props: props || {},
      children: children,
      generatedId : id++
    }
  : tag(props, children)
}
```

Please note that for the JSX to call our h function, we would have left the following comment:

```
/** @jsx h */
```

This is read by the JSX parser and the h function is called.

The app function contains various child functions that are explained in the sections that follow. These functions are built using functional programming concepts we have already learned. Each function accepts an input, acts on it, and returns a new state. The transformer (i.e., h function) receives tags and properties. This function is invoked by the

JSX parser, typically once they parse the JSX and send across the tag and properties as arguments. If we look closely at the h function, it uses the fundamental functional programming paradigm, recursion. It recursively builds the tree structure of DOM in JavaScript data type.

For example, calling h('buttons', props) where props is an object carrying other properties attached to the tag like onclick function, the function h would return a JSON equivalent as shown here.

```
{
children:["Increase"]
generatedId:1
props:{onclick: ƒ}
tag:"button"
}
```

CreateActions

The createActions function creates an array of functions, one each for action. The actions object is passed in as a parameter as shown earlier. Notice the usage of Object.Keys, closures, and the map function here. Each object within the actions array is a function that can be identified by its name. Each such function has access to the parent's variable scope (withActions), a closure. The closure when executed retains the values in the parent scope even though the function createAction has exited the execution context. The name of the function here in our example is up, down, and changeText.

```
function createActions(actions,withActions){
    Object.keys(withActions || {}).map(function(name){
        return actions[name] = function(data) {
            data = withActions[name];
            update(data)
        }
    }
```

```
    })
  return actions
}
```

Figure 11-5 is a sample of how the actions object looks during runtime.

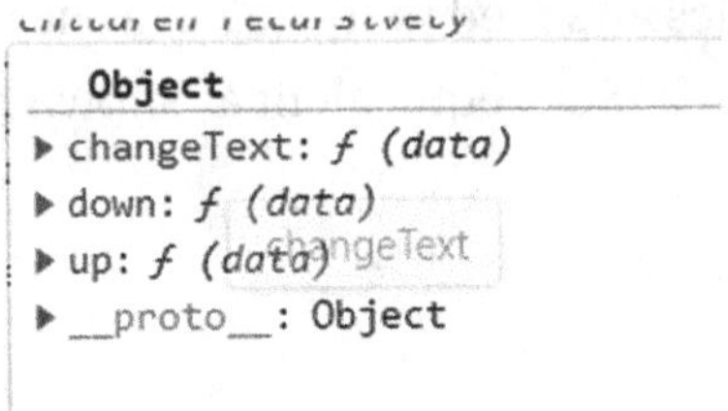

```
Object
▶ changeText: ƒ (data)
▶ down: ƒ (data)
▶ up: ƒ (data)
▶ __proto__: Object
```

Figure 11-5. *The actions object during runtime*

Render

The render function is responsible for replacing the old DOM with the new DOM.

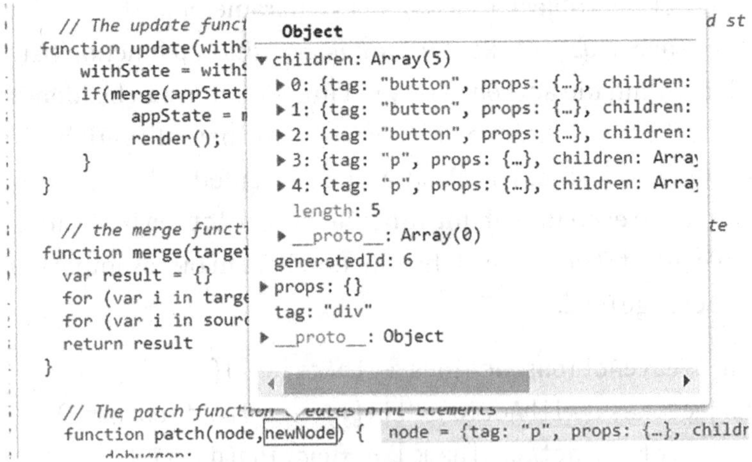

Figure 11-6. *The below image shows the state of Children Object during runtime*

```
function render() {
  let doc = patch(node,(node = appView(appState,appActions)))
  if(doc) {
      let children = document.body.children;
      for(let i = 0; i <= children.length; i++){
          removeElement(document.body, children[i],
          children[i])
      }
      document.body.appendChild(doc);
      }
}
```

Patch

The patch function is responsible for creating HTML nodes in recursion; for example, when patch receives the virtual DOM object, it creates the HTML equivalent of the node recursively.

```
function patch(node,newNode) {
        if (typeof newNode === "string") {
            let element = document.createTextNode(newNode)
          } else {
            let element = document.createElement(newNode.tag);
            for (let i = 0; i < newNode.children.length; ) {
                  element.appendChild(patch(node,newNode.
                  children[i++]))
            }
                for (let i in newNode.props) {
                  element[i] = newNode.props[i]
        }
```

```
            element.setAttribute("id",newNode.props.id !=
            undefined ? newNode.props.id : newNode.
            generatedId);
        }
    return element;
        }
}
```

Update

The update function is a higher order function responsible for updating the old state with a new state and rerendering the application. The update function is invoked when the user invokes an action like clicking any of the buttons shown in Figure 11-7.

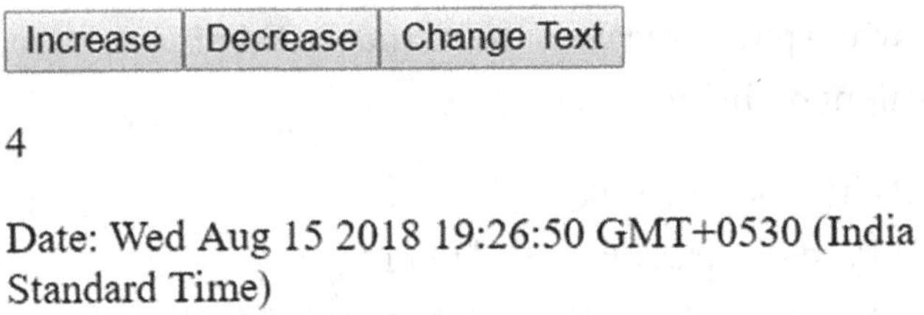

| Increase | Decrease | Change Text |

4

Date: Wed Aug 15 2018 19:26:50 GMT+0530 (India Standard Time)

Figure 11-7. *The below image shows the final UI for this example*

The update function receives a function as an argument; for example, up, down, or changeText, which makes it a higher order function. This gives us the benefit of adding dynamic behavior to the application. How? The update function is not aware of the argument with state until runtime, which leaves the app behavior to be decided during runtime based on what argument is passed. If up gets passed, the state is incremented; if down is passed, it is decremented. So much functionality with less code is the power of functional programming.

The current state of the application is passed on to your actions (example, up, down). Actions fundamentally follows the functional paradigm by returning a new state altogether. (Yes, HyperApp strictly follows the concepts of Redux, which in turn is fundamentally based on functional programming concepts.) This is done by the merge function. Once we get a new state, we will call the render function, as shown here.

```
function update(withState) {
    withState = withState(appState)
    if(merge(appState,withState)){
        appState = merge(appState,withState)
        render();
    }
  }
```

Merge

The merge function is a simple function that ensures the new state is merged with the old state.

```
function merge(target, source) {
    let result = {}
    for (let i in target) { result[i] = target[i] }
    for (let i in source) { result[i] = source[i] }
    return result
}
```

As you can see, where the state is altered, a new state that contains the old state and the state that has changed is created and altered. For example, if you invoke the Increase action, the merge ensures only the count property is updated. If you look closely, the merge function very closely resembles what Object.assign does; that is, it creates a new state from any given state by not affecting the given states. Hence we can also rewrite the merge function as shown here.

```
function merge(target, source) {
    let result = {}
    Object.assign(result, target, source)
    return result
}
```

That's the power of ES8 syntax.

Remove

The following functions are used to remove the children from the real DOM.

```
// remove element
function removeElement(parent, element, node) {
    function done() {
      parent.removeChild(removeChildren(element, node))
    }

    let cb = node.attributes && node.attributes.onremove
    if (cb) {
      cb(element, done)
    } else {
      done()
    }
}
// remove children recursively
function removeChildren(element, node) {
    let attributes = node.attributes
    if (attributes) {
```

```
    for (let i = 0; i < node.children.length; i++) {
        removeChildren(element.childNodes[i], node.children[i])
    }
}
    return element
}
```

The UI of the application looks like Figure 11-8. Increase, Decrease, and ChangeText are the actions, the number is 5, and Date is the state.

Increase	Decrease	Change Text

5

Date: Mon Jun 18 2018 01:38:24 GMT+0530 (India Standard Time)

Figure 11-8. *The below image shows the final UI for this example*

The source code of the library is available under hyperapp.js of the checkout branch. You can copy paste it into a new JS Fiddle to create the application (remember to select the correct language as explained earlier). You can also fork from my JS Fiddle at https://jsfiddle.net/vishwanathsrikanth/akhbj9r8/70/.

With this, we are finished building our second library. Clearly our library is much smaller than 1 KB, yet it is capable of building interactive web apps. Both the libraries that we built are based only on functions. All these functions work only on the input, rather than on global state. Functions use concepts like higher order functions to make the system easier to maintain. We see how each function receives input on time and works only with that input, returning a new state or function. We reused many higher order functions like map, each, assign, and so on. This shows how well-defined functions can be reused within our code base.

Also, both of these codes are taken from Redux and HyperApp (with tweaking of course), but you can see how popular libraries can be built by just following the functional concepts. It's all about functions at the end of the day!

Try to build more libraries like these using the functional JavaScript concepts explained in this book.

Summary

In this chapter we learned to use functional JavaScript concepts to build a library. We have learned how distributed state will disrupt the application's maintainability and predictability over time and how Redux-like frameworks can help us centralize state. Redux is a state container with a centralized read-only state; the state change is only allowed by reducers by passing actions and the old state. We also built a Redux-like library and an HTML application using functional JavaScript concepts. We learned about Virtual DOM and how it helps reduce DOM manipulations, and JSX syntax that can be used to represent DOM in JavaScript files. JSX and Virtual DOM concepts are used in building a library like HyperApp, the thinnest library available to build single-page applications.

CHAPTER 12

Testing and Closing Thoughts

All code is guilty, until proven innocent.

—Anonymous

We have covered most of the concepts surrounding functional JavaScript. We have learned the fundamentals, advanced ideas, and the latest concepts in the ES8 specification. Is our learning complete? Can we strongly assert that we have written workable code? No; unless the code is tested, no code is complete.

In this concluding chapter we learn to author tests for the functional JavaScript code we have written thus far. We will learn to use the industry's best testing frameworks and coding patterns for authoring flexible, easy-to-learn, automated tests. The patterns and practices discussed in this chapter can be used to test any functional code for all possible scenarios. We will also learn to test code that uses advanced JavaScript like Promises and asynchronous methods. The remainder of the chapter deals with using various tools for running tests, reporting test status, calculating code coverage, and applying linting to enforce better coding standards. Finally, we wrap up with some concluding thoughts for this second edition.

© Anto Aravinth, Srikanth Machiraju 2018
A. Aravinth and S. Machiraju, *Beginning Functional JavaScript*,
https://doi.org/10.1007/978-1-4842-4087-8_12

> **Note**   The chapter examples and library source code are in branch
> chap12. The repo's URL is https://github.com/antsmartian/
> functional-es8.git.
>
> Once you check out the code, please check out branch chap12:
>
> git checkout -b chap12 origin/chap12
>
> Open the command prompt as administrator, navigate to the folder that
> contains package.json, and run
>
> npm install
>
> to download the packages required for the code to run.

Introduction

Every developer should know that writing a test case is the only way to
certify the code runs and ensure there are no buggy paths. The tests are of
many kinds—unit, integration, performance, security/penetration, and so
on—each satisfying some certain criteria of the code. Which tests to author
depends completely on the function and priority of the functionality: It
is all about return on investment (ROI). Your tests should answer these
questions: Is this functionality important for the application? Will I be able
to certify this functionality works if I write this test? The core functionality
of the application is covered by all the previously mentioned tests,
whereas rarely used features might only need unit and integration tests.
Evangelizing unit tests is not going to be the gist of this section. Instead we
will learn the importance of authoring automated unit tests in the current
DevOps scenario.

DevOps (Development + Operations) is a set of processes, people,
and tools together used to define and ensure continuous frictionless
delivery of software applications. Now where does testing fit into this

model? The answer lies within continuous testing. Every high-performing Agile team with a DevOps delivery model should ensure they follow practices like continuous integration, testing, and delivery. In simple terms, every code check-in done by a developer is integrated into the one single repository, all the tests are run automatically, and the latest code is deployed automatically (provided the tests' passing criteria are met) to a staging environment. Having a flexible, reliable, and fast delivery pipeline is the key to success for the most successful companies as shown in Table 12-1.

Table 12-1. *Delivery Pipelines of Successful Companies*

Organization	Deployments
Facebook	2 deployments per day
Amazon	Deploys every 11.6 seconds
Netflix	1,000 times a day

Source: Wikipedia.

Let's say you are part of an Agile team that is building an application using Node, you have authored lot of code using best practices explained in this book, and now it is your responsibility to also write tests for your code so that it reaches acceptable code coverage and pass criteria. Teaching you how to author tests for the JavaScript functions is the aim of this chapter.

Figure 12-1 shows where the continuous testing phase sits in the overall application life cycle.

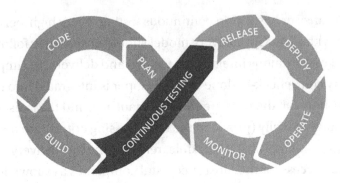

Figure 12-1. *The continuous testing phase of the application life cycle*

Types of Testing

The following are the most important categories of tests.

- *Unit tests:* Unit tests are written to test every function in isolation. This is going to be the primary focus of this chapter. Unit tests test individual functions by supplying input and making sure the output matches what is expected. Unit tests mock dependent behavior. More on mocking follows later in this chapter.

- *Integration tests:* Integration tests are written to test end-to-end functionality. For example, for a user registration scenario this test might go ahead and create a user in the data store and ensure it exists.

- *UI (functional tests):* UI tests are for web applications; these tests are written to control the browser and enact user journeys.

Other types of tests are smoke tests, regression tests, acceptance tests, system tests, preflight tests, penetration tests, and performance tests.

There are various frameworks available for authoring the tests in these categories, but explanation of these test types is beyond the scope of this book. This chapter deals only with unit tests.

BDD and TDD

Before we delve into the JavaScript test frameworks, let us briefly introduce the most notable test development methodologies, behavioral-driven development (BDD) and test-driven development (TDD).

BDD suggests testing the behavior of the function instead of its implementation. For example, consider the following function that just increments a given number by 1.

```
var mathLibrary = new MathLibrary();
var result = mathLibrary.increment(10)
```

BDD advises the test to be written as shown next. Although this looks like a simple unit test, there is a subtle difference. Here we are not worried about the implementation logic (like the initial value of Sum).

```
var expectedValue = mathlibrary.seed + 10;
// imagine seed is a property of MathLibrary
Assert.equal(result, expectedValue);
```

Assertions are functions that help us verify the actual value against the expected value or vice versa. Here, we are not worried over the implementation details; rather, we assert the behavior of the function, which is to increment the value by 1. If the value of the seed changes tomorrow, we do not have to update the function.

Note   Assert is part of the nomenclature in most testing frameworks. It is used primarily to compare expected vs. actual in a variety of ways.

TDD suggests you write the test first. For example, in the current scenario we write the following test first. Of course it would fail because there is no `MathLibrary` or its corresponding function called `increment`.

```
Assert.equal(MathLibrary.increment(10), 11);
```

The idea behind TDD is to write assertions first that satisfy the functional requirement and that would initially fail. Development progresses by making necessary corrections (writing code) to pass the test.

JavaScript Test Frameworks

JavaScript being a vastly adapted language for writing functional code, there are numerous test frameworks available, including Mocha, Jest (by Facebook), Jasmine, and Cucumber, to name a few. The most famous among them are Mocha and Jasmine. To write a unit test for JavaScript functions we need the libraries or tools that can cover the following basic needs.

- Test structure, which defines the folder structure, file names, and corresponding configuration.

- Assertion functions, a library that can be used to assert with flexibility.

- Reporter, a framework for displaying the results in various formats like Console, HTML, JSON, or XML.

- Mocks, a framework that can provide test doubles to fake dependent components.

- Code coverage, so the framework should be able to clearly tell the number of lines or functions covered with tests.

Unfortunately, no one testing framework provides all of these functionalities. For example, Mocha does not have an assertion library. Fortunately, most frameworks like Mocha and Jasmine are extensible; we can use Babel's assertion library or expect.js with Mocha for performing clean assertions. Between Mocha and Jasmine, we will be writing Mocha tests as we feel it is more flexible than Jasmine. Of course we will also see a glimpse of Jasmine tests at the end of this section.

Note   At the time of writing Jasmine does not support tests for ES8 features, which is one of the reasons for the bias toward Mocha.

Testing Using Mocha

The following sections explain how to set up Mocha for authoring tests and the nitty-gritty of authoring sync and async tests with mocking. Let's get started.

Installation

Mocha (https://mochajs.org) is a community-backed, feature-rich JavaScript test framework that can run on both Node.js and browsers. Mocha boasts of making asynchronous testing simple and fun, which we will witness in a moment.

Install Mocha globally and for the development environment as shown here.

```
npm install –global mocha
npm install –save-dev mocha
```

Add a new folder called `test` and add a new file within the `test` folder called `mocha-tests.js`. The following is the updated file structure.

```
| functional-playground
|------play.js
| lib
|------es8-functional.js
| test
| -----mocha-tests.js
```

Simple Mocha Test

Add the following simple Mocha test to `mocha-tests.js`.

```
var assert = require('assert');
describe('Array', function () {
    describe('#indexOf()', function () {
        it('should return -1 when the value is not present',
        function () {
            assert.equal(-1, [1, 2, 3].indexOf(4));
        });
    });
});
```

Let's understand this bit by bit. The first line of code is required to import the Babel assertion library. As mentioned earlier, Mocha doesn't have an out-of-the-box assertion library so this line is required. You can also use any other assertion library like `expect.js`, `chai.js`, `should.js`, or many more.

```
var assert = require('assert');
```

Mocha tests are hierarchical in nature. The first `describe` function shown earlier describes the first test category `'Array'`. Each primary category can have multiple describes, like '#indexOf'. Here '#indexOf' is a subcategory that contains the tests related to the indexOf function of the array. The actual test starts with the it keyword. The first parameter of the it function should always describe the expected behavior (Mocha uses BDD).

```
it('should return -1 when the value is not present', function(){})
```

There can be multiple it functions within a subcategory. The following code is used to assert the expected vs. actual. There can also be multiple asserts in a single test case (the it function here is a single test case). By default, the test stops at the first failure in case of multiple asserts, but this behavior can be altered.

The following code is added to package.json for running the Mocha tests. Also check the dev dependencies and dependencies section when you check out the branch to understand the support libraries that are pulled in.

```
"mocha": "mocha --compilers js:babel-core/register --require babel-polyfill",
```

The switches –compilers and –require here are optional; in this case they are used to compile ES8 code. Running the following command runs the tests.

```
npm run mocha
```

Figure 12-2 shows a sample response.

```
> learning-functional@1.0.0 mocha C:\code\apress\code\functional-es6
> mocha --compilers js:babel-core/register --require babel-polyfill


(node:7896) DeprecationWarning: "--compilers" will be removed in a futur
or more info
  Array
    #indexOf()
      √ should return -1 when the value is not present


  1 passing (12ms)
```

Figure 12-2. *Sample response to switches*

Observe the way test results are presented. `Array` is the first level in the hierarchy, followed by `#indexOf` and then the actual test result. The statement **1 passing** above shows the summary of tests.

Tests for Currying, Monads, and Functors

We have learned a lot of functional programming concepts like currying, functors, and monads. In this section we learn to write tests for the concepts we learned earlier.

Let's start by authoring unit tests for currying, the process of converting a function with *n* number of arguments into a nested unary function. Well, that's the formal definition, but it will probably not help us author unit tests. Authoring unit tests for any function is quite easy. The first step is to list its primary feature set. Here we are referring to the `curryN` function we wrote in Chapter 6. Let's define its behavior

1. CurryN should always return a function.

2. CurryN should only accept functions, and passing any other value should throw an error.

3. CurryN function should return the same value as
    that of a normal function when called with the same
    number of arguments.

Now, let us start writing tests for these features.

```
it("should return a function", function(){
        let add = function(){}
        assert.equal(typeof curryN(add), 'function');
});
```

This test will assert if curryN always returns a function object.

```
it("should throw if a function is not provided", function(){
        assert.throws(curryN, Error);
    });
```

This test will ensure that curryN throws Error when a function is not
passed.

```
it("calling curried function and original function with same
arguments should return the same value", function(){
        let multiply = (x,y,z) => x * y * z;

        let curriedMultiply = curryN(multiply);
        assert.equal(curriedMultiply(1,2,3), multiply(1,2,3));
        assert.equal(curriedMultiply(1)(2)(3), multiply(1,2,3));
        assert.equal(curriedMultiply(1)(2,3), multiply(1,2,3));

        curriedMultiply = curryN(multiply)(2);
        assert.equal(curriedMultiply(1,3), multiply(1,2,3));
    });
```

The preceding test can be used to test the basic functionality of a
curried function. Now let's write some tests for functors. Before that, like
we did for currying, let's review the features of a functor.

1. A functor is a container that holds a value.

2. A functor is a plain object that implements the function map.

3. A functor like MayBe should handle null or undefined.

4. A functor like MayBe should chain.

Now, based on how we defined the functor let's see some tests.

```
it("should store the value", function(){
        let testValue = new Container(3);
        assert.equal(testValue.value, 3);
    });
```

This test asserts that a functor like container holds a value. Now, how do you test if the functor implements map? There are couple of ways: You can assert on the prototype or call the function and expect a correct value, as shown here.

```
it("should implement map", function(){
        let double = (x) => x + x;
        assert.equal(typeof Container.of(3).map == 'function', true)
        let testValue = Container.of(3).map(double).map(double);
        assert.equal(testValue.value, 12);
    });
```

The following tests assert if the function handles null and is capable of chaining.

```
it("may be should handle null", function(){
        let upperCase = (x) => x.toUpperCase();
        let testValue = MayBe.of(null).map(upperCase);
        assert.equal(testValue.value, null);
    });
```

```
it("may be should chain", function(){
    let upperCase = (x) => x.toUpperCase();
    let testValue = MayBe.of("Chris").map(upperCase).
    map((x) => "Mr." + x);
    assert.equal(testValue.value, "Mr.CHRIS");
});
```

Now, with this approach it should be easy to write tests for monads. Where do you start? Here is a little help: Let's see if you can author tests for the following rules by yourself.

1. Monads should implement join.

2. Monads should implement chain.

3. Monads should remove nesting.

If you need help, check out chap12 branch from the GitHub URL.

Testing Functional Library

We have authored many functions in the es-functional.js library and used play.js to execute them. In this section we learn how to author tests for the functional JavaScript code we have written so far. Like play.js, before using the functions they should be imported in the file mocha-tests.js, so add the following line to the mocha-tests.js file.

```
import { forEach, Sum } from "../lib/es8-functional.js";
```

The following code shows the Mocha tests written for JavaScript functions.

```
describe('es8-functional', function () {
    describe('Array', function () {
        it('Foreach should double the elements of Array, when
        double function is passed', function () {
            var array = [1, 2, 3];
```

```
    const doublefn = (data) => data * 2;
    forEach(array, doublefn);
    assert.equal(array[0], 1)
  });
  it('Sum should sum up elements of array', function () {
    var array = [1, 2, 3];
    assert.equal(Sum(array), 6)
  });
  it('Sum should sum up elements of array including
  negative values', function () {
    var array = [1, 2, 3, -1];
    assert.notEqual(Sum(array), 6)
  });
});
```

Async Tests with Mocha

Surprise, surprise! Mocha also supports async and await, and it is suprisingly simple to test Promises or async functions as shown here.

```
describe('Promise/Async', function () {
  it('Promise should return es8', async function (done) {
    done();
    var result = await fetchTextByPromise();
    assert.equal(result, 'es8');
  })
});
```

Notice the call to done here. Without the call to the done function, the test will time out because it does not wait for 2 s as required by our promise. The done function here notifies the Mocha framework. Run the tests again using the following command.

```
npm run mocha
```

The results are shown in Figure 12-3.

```
> learning-functional@1.0.0 mocha C:\code\apress\code\functional-es6
> mocha --compilers js:babel-core/register --require babel-polyfill


(node:17256) DeprecationWarning: "--compilers" will be removed in a future version of
for more info
  Array
    #indexOf()
      √ should return -1 when the value is not present

  es6-functional
    Array
      √ Foreach should double the elements of Array, when double function is passed
      √ Sum should sum up elements of array
      √ Sum should sum up elements of array including negative values
    Promise/Async
      √ Promise should return es8


  5 passing (72ms)
```

Figure 12-3. *The below image shows the test results*

Reiterating the opening statement, Mocha might be initially very hard to set up due to its inherent flexibility adhering to the fact that it gels well with almost any framework for authoring fine unit tests, but at the end of the day, the rewards are profuse.

Mocking Using Sinon

Let's say you are part of Team A, which is part of a large Agile team divided into smaller teams like Team A, Team B, and Team C. Larger Agile teams usually are divided by business requirements or geographical regions. Let us say Team B consumes Teams C's library and Team A uses Team B's functional library and each team is expected to hand over thoroughly tested code. As a developer from Team A, while consuming Team B's functions would you author tests again? No. Then how would you ensure your code is working when you are dependent on calling Team B's functions? This is where mocking libraries come into the picture and Sinon is one such library. As mentioned earlier, Mocha doesn't come with a mocking library out of the box, but it seamlessly integrates with Sinon.

Sinon (Sinonjs.org) is a stand-alone framework that provides spies, stubs, and mocks for JavaScript. Sinon integrates with any test framework easily.

Note   Spies, mocks, or stubs, although they solve a similar problem and sound related, have subtle differences that are critical to understand. We recommend learning the differences between fakes, mocks, and stubs in greater detail. This section provides only a summary.

A fake imitates any JavaScript object like a function or object. Consider the following function.

```
var testObject= {};

testObject.doSomethingTo10 = (func) => {
    const x = 10;
    return func(x);
}
```

This code takes a function and runs it on constant 10. The following code shows how to test this function using Sinon fakes.

```
it("doSomethingTo10", function () {
    const fakeFunction = sinon.fake();
    testObject.doSomethingTo10(fakeFunction);
    assert.equal(fakeFunction.called, true);
});
```

As you can see we have not created an actual function to act on 10; instead we faked a function. It is important to assert the fake, hence the statement `assert.equal (fakeFunction.called, true)` ensures the fake function is called, which asserts the behavior of the function doSomethingTo10. Sinon provides more comprehensive ways to test the behavior of fake within the context of the test function. See the documentation for more details.

Consider this function:

```
testObject.tenTimes = (x) => 10 * x;
```

The following code shows a test case written using Sinon's stub. As you notice, a stub can be used to define the behavior of the function.

```
it("10 Times", function () {
        const fakeFunction = sinon.stub(testObject, "tenTimes");
        fakeFunction.withArgs(10).returns(10);
        var result = testObject.tenTimes(10);
        assert.equal(result, 10);
        assert.notEqual(result, 0);
    });
```

More often we write code that interacts with external dependencies like HTTP Call. As mentioned earlier, unit tests are light scoped, and the external dependencies should be mocked, in this case the HTTP Call.

Let's say we have the following functions:

```
var httpLibrary = {};
function httpGetAsync(url,callback) {
    // HTTP Get Call to external dependency
}
```

```
httpLibrary.httpGetAsync = httpGetAsync;
httpLibrary.getAsyncCaller = function (url, callback) {
  try {
      const response = httpLibrary.httpGetAsync(url, function
      (response) {
          if (response.length > 0) {
              for (let i = 0; i < response.length; i++) {
                  httpLibrary.usernames += response[i].username +
                  ",";
              }
              callback(httpLibrary.usernames)
          }
      });
  } catch (error) {
      throw error
  }
}
```

If you would like to test only getAsyncCaller without getting into the nitty-gritty of httpGetAsync (let's say it is developed by Team B), we can use Sinon mocks as shown here.

```
it("Mock HTTP Call", function () {
    const getAsyncMock = sinon.mock(httpLibrary);
    getAsyncMock.expects("httpGetAsync").once().returns(null);
    httpLibrary.getAsyncCaller("", (usernames) =>
    console.log(usernames));
    getAsyncMock.verify();
    getAsyncMock.restore();
});
```

This test case makes sure while testing getAsyncCaller, httpGetAsync is mocked. The following test case tests the same method without using mock.

```
it("HTTP Call", function () {
  httpLibrary.getAsyncCaller("https://jsonplaceholder.
  typicode.com/users");
});
```

Before I wrap up writing tests for functional JavaScript code, let me show how to write tests using Jasmine.

Testing with Jasmine

Jasmine (https://jasmine.github.io) is also a famous testing framework; in fact, the APIs of Jasmine and Mocha are similar. Jasmine is the most widely used framework when building applications with AngularJS (or Angular). Unlike Mocha, Jasmine comes with a built-in assertion library. The only troublesome area with Jasmine at the point of writing was testing asynchronous code. Let's learn to set up Jasmine in our code in the next few steps.

```
npm install –save-dev jasmine
```

If you intend to install it globally, run this command:

```
npm install -g jasmine
```

Jasmine dictates a test structure including a configuration file, so running the following command will set up the test's structure.

```
./node_modules/.bin/jasmine init
```

That command creates the following folder structure:

```
|-Spec
|-----Support
|---------jasmine.json (Jasmine configuration file)
```

Jasmine.json contains the test configuration; for example, spec_dir is used to specify the folder in which to look for Jasmine tests, and spec_files describes the common keyword that is used to identify test files. For more configuration details, please visit https://jasmine.github.io/2.3/node.html#section-Configuration.

Let's create a Jasmine test file in the spec folder that is created with the init command and name the file jasmine-tests-spec.js. (Remember without the keyword spec our test file will not be located by Jasmine.)

The following code shows a sample Jasmine test.

```
import { forEach, Sum, fetchTextByPromise } from "../lib/es8-functional.js";
import 'babel-polyfill';

describe('Array', function () {
    describe('#indexOf()', function () {
        it('should return -1 when the value is not present',
            function () {
                expect([1, 2, 3].indexOf(4)).toBe(-1);
            });
    });
});

describe('es8-functional', function () {
    describe('Array', function () {
        it('Foreach should double the elements of Array, when
            double function is passed', function () {
                var array = [1, 2, 3];
```

```
        const doublefn = (data) => data * 2;
        forEach(array, doublefn);
        expect(array[0]).toBe(1)
    });
});
```

As you can see, the code looks very similar to Mocha tests except for the assertions. You can rebuild the test library entirely using Jasmine, and we leave it up to you to figure out how to do so.

The following command is added to package.json to execute Jasmine tests.

```
"jasmine": "jasmine"
```

Running the following command executes the tests:

```
npm run jasmine
```

```
C:\code\apress\code\functional-es6>npm run jasmine

> learning-functional@1.0.0 jasmine C:\code\apress\code\functional-es6
> jasmine

Randomized with seed 56566
Started
.....


5 specs, 0 failures
Finished in 0.06 seconds
Randomized with seed 56566 (jasmine --random=true --seed=56566)
```

Figure 12-4. *The below image shows test results using Jasmine*

Code Coverage

How sure are we that we have covered the critical areas with the tests? Well for any language the code coverage is the only metric that can explain the code covered by tests. JavaScript is no exception, as we can get the number of lines or percentage of our code covered by tests.

Istanbul (`https://gotwarlost.github.io/istanbul/`) is one of the best known frameworks that can calculate the code coverage for JavaScript at the statement, Git branch, or function level. Setting up Istanbul is easy. nyc is the name of the command-line argument that can be used to get code coverage, so let us run this command to install nyc:

```
npm install -g --save-dev nyc
```

The following command can be used to run Mocha tests with code coverage, so let us add it to `package.json`.

```
"mocha-cc": "nyc mocha --compilers js:babel-core/register
--require babel-polyfill"
```

Run the following command to run the Mocha tests and also get the code coverage.

```
npm run mocha-cc
```

The results are shown in Figure 12-5.

```
9 passing (156ms)

-------------------|----------|----------|----------|----------|--------------------|
File               | % Stmts  | % Branch | % Funcs  | % Lines  | Uncovered Line #s  |
-------------------|----------|----------|----------|----------|--------------------|
All files          |   93.94  |    50    |   90.91  |   93.75  |                    |
 es6-functional.js |   93.94  |    50    |   90.91  |   93.75  |              20,57 |
-------------------|----------|----------|----------|----------|--------------------|
```

Figure 12-5. _The below image shows code coverage for tests written using Mocha_

As you can see, we are 93% covered except lines 20 and 57 from the file `es8-functional.js`. The ideal percentage of code coverage depends on several factors, all accounting for return on investment. Most commonly 85% is a recommended number, but lesser than that will also work if the code is covered by any other tests.

Linting

Code analysis is as important as code coverage, especially in larger teams. Code analysis helps you impose uniform coding rules, follow best practices, and enforce best practices for readability and maintainability. JavaScript code we have written so far might not adhere to best practices, as this is more applicable to production code. In this section let's see how to apply coding rules to functional JavaScript code.

ESLint (https://eslint.org/) is a command-line tool for identifying incorrect coding patterns in ECMAScript/JavaScript. It is relatively easy to install ESLint into any new or existing project. The following command installs ESLint.

```
npm install --save-dev -g eslint
```

ESLint is configuration driven, and the command that follows creates a default configuration. You might have to answer a few questions as shown in Figure 12-6 here. For this coding sample we are using coding rules recommended by Google.

```
eslint --init
```

```
C:\code\apress\code\functional-es6>eslint --init
? How would you like to configure ESLint? (Use arrow keys)
> Answer questions about your style
  Use a popular style guide
  Inspect your JavaScript file(s)
```

Figure 12-6. *The below image shows eslinit initialization steps*

Here is the sample configuration file.

```
{
    "parserOptions": {
        "ecmaVersion": 6,
        "sourceType": "module"
    },
    "rules": {
        "semi": ["error", "always"],
        "quotes": ["error", "double"]
    },
    "env": {
        "node": true
    }
}
```

Let's look at the first rule.

```
"semi": ["error", "always"],
```

This rule says a semicolon is mandatory after every statement. Now if we run it against the code file es-functional.js we have written so far, we get the results shown in Figure 12-7. As you can see, we violated this rule in many places. Imposing coding rules or guidelines should be done at the very beginning of the project. Introducing coding rules or adding new rules after accumulating a huge code base results in an enormous amount of code debt, which will be difficult to handle.

```
C:\code\apress\code\functional-es6>eslint lib\es6-functional.js

C:\code\apress\code\functional-es6\lib\es6-functional.js
   2:23   error   Strings must use doublequote   quotes
   8:2    error   Missing semicolon              semi
  15:2    error   Missing semicolon              semi
  23:2    error   Missing semicolon              semi
  30:22   error   Strings must use doublequote   quotes
  31:23   error   Strings must use doublequote   quotes
  34:23   error   Strings must use doublequote   quotes
  35:44   error   Missing semicolon              semi
  36:31   error   Missing semicolon              semi
  37:13   error   Missing semicolon              semi
  53:46   error   Missing semicolon              semi
  57:18   error   Missing semicolon              semi
  59:2    error   Missing semicolon              semi
  61:57   error   Missing semicolon              semi

✖ 14 problems (14 errors, 0 warnings)
  14 errors, 0 warnings potentially fixable with the `--fix` option.
```

Figure 12-7. *The below image shows the result from eslint tool*

ESLint helps you fix these errors. As suggested earlier, you just have to run this command:

```
eslint lib\es8-functional.js  --fix
```

All errors are gone! You might not be lucky all the time, so ensure you impose restrictions early in the development phase.

Unit Testing Library Code

In the previous chapter we learned to create libraries that can help build applications. A good library is one that is testable, so the more the code coverage of your tests, the higher the likelihood consumers can trust your code. Tests help quickly check your code for affected areas when you change something. In this section we author Mocha tests for the Redux library code we have written in the previous chapter.

The following code is available in the mocha-test.js file. The mocha-test.js file refers to the code from our Redux library. The following test ensures that initially the state is always empty.

```
it('is empty initially', () => {
        assert.equal(store.getState().counter, 0);
    });
```

One of the main functions in our library was to assert if actions can influence state change. In the following state we initiate state change by calling IncrementCounter, which is called when a click event is raised. IncrementCounter should increase the state by 1.

```
// test for state change once
    it('state change once', () => {
        global.document = null;
        incrementCounter();
        assert.equal(store.getState().counter, 1);
    });
```

```
// test for state change twice
    it('state change twice', () => {
        global.document = null;
        incrementCounter();
        assert.equal(store.getState().counter, 2);
    });
```

The last function we are going to assert is to check if there is at least one listener registered for state change. To ensure we have a listener we also register a listener; this is also called an Arrange phase.

```
// test for listener count
    it('minimum 1 listener', () => {
        //Arrange
        global.document = null;
        store.subscribe(function () {
            console.log(store.getState());
        });

        //Act
        var hasMinOnelistener = store.currentListeners.length > 1;

        //Assert
        assert.equal(hasMinOnelistener, true);
    });
```

You can run npm run mocha or npm run mocha-cc to execute the tests with code coverage. You will notice in Figure 12-8 that we have covered more than 80% of the code we have written in the library.

File	% Stmts	% Branch	% Funcs	% Lines	Uncovered Line #s
All files	88.33	50	85.71	88.14	
es6-functional.js	93.94	50	90.91	93.75	20,57
redux.js	81.48	50	80	81.48	51,71,73,74,75

Figure 12-8. *The below image shows the code coverage results*

With this experience it would be a good exercise to write unit tests for the HyperApp-like library we built in the previous chapter.

Closing Thoughts

Another wonderful journey comes to an end. We hope you had fun like we did learning new concepts and patterns in JavaScript functional programming. Here are some closing thoughts.

- If you're starting fresh on project, try to use the concepts used in this book. Each concept used in this book has a specific area of use. In going through a user scenario, analyze if you can use any of the explained concepts. For example, if you are making a REST API call, you would analyze if you can create a library to execute REST API calls asynchronously.

- If you're working on an existing project with lots of spaghetti JavaScript code, analyze the code to refactor some of it into reusable, testable functions. The best way to learn is by practice, so scan through your code, find loose ends, and stitch them together to make an extensible, testable, reusable JavaScript function.

- Stay tuned to ECMAScript updates, as ECMAScript will continue to mature and get better over time. You can watch for the proposals at `https://github.com/tc39/proposals` or if you have a new idea or thought that can improve ECMAScript or help developers, you can go ahead with the proposal.

Summary

In this chapter we learned the importance of tests, types of tests, and development models like BDD and TDD. We came to understand the requirements of a JavaScript testing framework and learned about the best known ones, Mocha and Jasmine. We authored simple tests, tests for a functional library, and async tests using Mocha. Sinon is a JavaScript mocking library that provides spies, stubs, and mocks for JavaScript. We learned how to integrate Sinon with Mocha to mock dependent behavior or objects. We also learned to use Jasmine to write tests for JavaScript functions. Istanbul integrates well with Mocha and provides us code coverage that can be used as a measure of reliability. Linting helps us write clean JavaScript code, and in this chapter we learned to define coding rules using ESLint.

Correction to: Fun with Functors

Anto Aravinth and Srikanth Machiraju

Correction to:

Chapter 8 in: A. Aravinth and S. Machiraju, *Beginning Functional JavaScript*: Uncover the Concepts of Functional Programming with EcmaScript 8
https://doi.org/10.1007/978-1-4842-4087-8_8

The original version of the chapter was inadvertently published with an incorrect code in chapter 8 and that has been corrected now.

The updated version of the chapter can be found at
https://doi.org/10.1007/978-1-4842-4087-8_8

© Anto Aravinth, Srikanth Machiraju 2020
A. Aravinth and S. Machiraju, *Beginning Functional JavaScript*,
https://doi.org/10.1007/978-1-4842-4087-8_13

Index

© Anto Aravinth, Srikanth Machiraju 2018
A. Aravinth and S. Machiraju, *Beginning Functional JavaScript*,
https://doi.org/10.1007/978-1-4842-4087-8

U

V, W, X, Y, Z

Printed in the United States
by Bookmasters

Printed in the United States
By Bookmasters